*To each and every one of you.
You may open this book and put it back down again, or you may buy the book and dog-ear the pages, letting it become a part of your daily cooking. No matter who you are or what you do with this book, just remember you matter. xx*

Confidence in the KITCHEN

How to **FEED YOUR FAMILY, WOW YOUR GUESTS** *and* **MASTER THE PERFECT RED LIP!**

EMMYLOU MACCARTHY

plum. Pan Macmillan Australia

CONTENTS

EMMYLOU'S LIFE HACKS

HELLO!

If you're reading this, you may be someone who is already part of my online tribe, in which case, thank you for your ongoing support and belief in me! I cannot express how grateful I am for you – I wouldn't be able to spend my life living out my passions and I definitely wouldn't be here writing this book if it wasn't for you.

If you've never 'met' me, thank you for picking up this book. Let me introduce myself.

I am a producer, presenter and fashion stylist with a passion for body positivity and helping people to live their most confident lives. I am also a mum and partner and I share my whole life as honestly and openly as I possibly can via Instagram Stories. The members of my online community are my biggest supporters and are with me every step of the way. I feel incredibly grateful to be able to be so unapologetically myself and share things that inspire me and that I know will make the lives of my tribe a little bit easier. I have produced and presented many events, as well as my own television show, appeared at food festivals sharing my easy entertaining ideas, and given keynote speeches at conferences on self confidence and living your best life.

My passion for food and cooking set in when I was very young. My mum is a Vietnamese immigrant who came to raise a family in Australia after the war. She found connection and community through sharing her food and culture and this has had a powerful impact on my life. I spent my childhood cooking alongside her, learning both modern and traditional techniques, figuring out how to balance flavours and discovering the joy of sharing homemade food with the people you love.

Mum cooked from a huge collection of recipe books, including traditional Vietnamese books as well as the classic *Women's Weekly* cookbooks that many of my friends' mums also had. She collected recipes clipped from magazines in doctors' waiting rooms and was always excited to try new, creative dishes from all over the world. It was inspiring to see her enthusiasm for new foods and I always loved watching her create meals that looked and smelled glorious and that seemed to have the power to overcome conflicts and bring our family together around the dinner table.

She was (and is) a magnificent entertainer, bringing together friends to have fun, share food and make memories. Some of my fondest childhood memories are of watching my mum play tennis at the local club. She would prepare a killer tray of sandwiches for the ladies to enjoy and she became part of a close-knit community through sharing her love of food and sport. It was inspiring watching her, a Vietnamese woman in Australia (at a time when Vietnam was less than popular with many westerners), connect and make close friends by, ironically, sharing her culture.

My father, the son of an Irish adventurer, who grew up in Kenya, also had a great influence on me. He shared his love of music (the sound track to my young life was a retro mix of Jimi Hendrix, Paul Simon, Nina Simone, The Beatles, The Rolling Stones and, as I got older, The Red Hot Chilli Peppers), appetite for adventure and travel and his respect for discipline and hard work, developed through his many years of martial arts. As a second-degree black belt in tae kwon do, he was the right-hand man of the club founder, Mr Shimboo Kim, a Korean legend in the tae kwon do world. Mr Kim built a strong community who enjoyed gathering for parties and, more often than not, those get-togethers took place at our house.

My siblings and I would sit at the window and watch with excitement as the cars arrived. They would park on the street, nature strip, anywhere they could fit, and families would walk in with kids and eskies in tow. The parties were always BYO drinks and meats and mum would make all the salads. Mum would ask everyone to bring a small fruit salad as well, which was a great trick of hers – she would get all the fruit salads and mix them up in one big bowl, making an exotic and glorious fruit medley that she served with ice cream and whipped cream. I would gather all the kids together and organise plays and shows that we would present to our parents. Organising fabulous performances for people to enjoy was my thing back then and it still is today.

These parties were known for going well into the night and they were, without a doubt, where my love of community and passion for entertaining originated. Like my mum, I use food to bring people together and share the love I have for family. I have written this book to bring together my most-requested recipes, hints and tips to make it easier to cook for your family and friends. I share some delicious weeknight meals (that your kids will actually eat!), make it simple for you to wow your friends with impressive (but super easy) dishes and show you how to create an epic grazing table for your next party. Some of these recipes could be described as kitsch. You know the ones I'm talking about – cobb loaf, sausage rolls, potato salad. But these recipes have stood the test of time for a reason – they're bloody delicious! I want you to walk into that barbecue with your head (and cobb loaf!) held high. Be proud! Be confident! Cooking should be fun, but it should also come from the heart. I want you to fall in love with entertaining, and I hope these recipes help make that happen.

Perhaps you picked up this book because you are looking for simple, delicious recipes, or maybe you need some ideas on how to throw a dinner party with fun and flair. Whatever your reason, I hope you absolutely love it. If you do, please share it on Insta and tag me as I LOVE hearing from my tribe!

Love
Emmylou xxx

‘I am grate
to share thi
make your

to be able
s I know will
ves easier!’

WEEKNIGHT FAVOURITES

Stuff your kids will actually eat!

These days it seems like everyone has a recipe for pork and fennel sausage rolls. Mine's not the first, nor will it be the last. But is it the best? Yeah, maybe! Especially if the response from my Insta tribe is anything to go by! You guys are constantly raving about these sausage rolls, usually after you've served them at a kids' party. They're a great way to sneak a few veggies into their diet and kids love the sweetness of the apple.

Pork and fennel SAUSAGE ROLLS

Makes 36 small sausage rolls

500 g pork mince
1 zucchini, grated and finely chopped
1 carrot, grated and finely chopped
1 small red apple, cored and grated
handful of flat-leaf parsley leaves, chopped (optional)
sea salt and freshly ground black pepper
3 sheets frozen puff pastry, thawed and cut in half
1 egg, lightly beaten
2 teaspoons fennel seeds, lightly toasted
tomato sauce, to serve (optional)

tip

If you don't want to cook all the sausage rolls at once, wrap them tightly in baking paper and foil and pop them in the freezer for up to 3 months. Unwrap and cook them in the oven from frozen in a preheated 180°C oven for 30 minutes or until cooked through and golden.

Preheat the oven to 180°C and line a baking tray with baking paper.

Place the pork, zucchini, carrot, apple and parsley (if using) in a large bowl. Season well with salt and pepper and mix well with your hands.

Divide the pork mixture into six equal portions. Place one portion evenly along the longest edge of a pastry sheet, shaping it with a spoon or your fingers. Roll the pastry over to enclose the filling, then brush a little egg along the pastry edge and press to seal. Trim off the excess pastry and repeat with the remaining filling and pastry to make six logs.

Slice six indents into the top of each log (without cutting all the way through) – this will help the logs cook evenly, releasing steam while keeping all the moisture in. Brush with the remaining beaten egg and transfer to the prepared tray. Sprinkle over the fennel seeds and bake for 20 minutes or until the filling is cooked and the pastry is puffed and golden.

Cut each log into six sausage rolls, using the indents as a guide, and serve warm with some tomato sauce, if desired.

I don't have much to say about this recipe, guys. It's a bloody quiche! Bacon, eggs, cream – done. Once you've made it a couple of times you won't even need to look at the recipe. It's a great dish to bake to take to someone, and only takes about ten minutes to whip up. Just make sure you bake an extra one for yourself!

Old-school QUICHE

Serves 6–8

2 sheets frozen puff pastry, thawed
250 g rindless bacon rashers, chopped
handful of flat-leaf parsley leaves, roughly chopped
2 spring onions, thinly sliced
large handful of baby spinach leaves, roughly chopped
125 g (1 cup) grated cheddar
4 eggs, lightly beaten
250 ml (1 cup) pouring cream

tip

Remove the puff pastry from the freezer before you prepare your ingredients. By the time you have chopped everything up, the pastry will have softened enough to line the tin easily.

For a vego version, swap the bacon for 150 g (1 cup) cubed roasted pumpkin or 65 g (½ cup) semi-dried tomatoes.

Preheat the oven to 180°C and line a 20 cm tart tin with baking paper. (I often use my cast-iron frying pan which also works really well.)

Lay one sheet of pastry in the base of the tin so the corners hang over the edge. Place the second sheet of pastry on top at a 45-degree angle and press the pastry into the tin – it should look like an eight-pointed star.

Combine all the remaining ingredients in a bowl. Pour the mixture into the pastry case and pop it in the oven for 15 minutes. Reduce the temperature to 160°C and bake for another 30 minutes or until the pastry is golden and the quiche is cooked through.

Set aside to cool slightly, then remove from the tin, slice and serve with your favourite garden salad.

I tried to think of a fancy name for this dish, but it's impossible. This is brown chicken. Always has been, always will be. It's my mum's recipe and she's been cooking it for as long as I can remember. When I was born she hardly spoke any English so she would have started calling it brown chicken because it's the logical choice. It's the sort of recipe you will cook forever. It has authentic Vietnamese flavours and the kids absolutely love it. I have four brothers and sisters and, without fail, it's the first thing we ask for whenever any of us visit our mum.

My mum's BROWN CHICKEN

Serves 4

1 tablespoon vegetable oil
1 onion, sliced
8 chicken chops, skin on
4 garlic cloves, crushed
1 tablespoon karamel masakan (see tip)
80 ml (⅓ cup) fish sauce
1½ tablespoons brown sugar

TO SERVE
steamed rice
your favourite steamed greens
sliced baby cucumber

tip

Karamel masakan (cooking caramel) can be found in Asian supermarkets and has recently started to appear on regular supermarket shelves, too.

Heat the oil in a large, deep frying pan over high heat, add the onion and cook for 2 minutes or until softened and lightly golden.

Pat the chicken dry with paper towel, then add to the pan, along with the garlic, and cook for 3 minutes on each side or until browned. Drizzle the cooking caramel over the chicken, then add the fish sauce, sugar and 150 ml of water and mix well.

Reduce the heat to medium–low and put the lid on, leaving a little gap for the steam to escape. Cook for 15 minutes, then turn the chicken over and cook for another 15 minutes.

Serve with steamed rice, your favourite greens and sliced cucumber.

QUICK CROISSANTS

One of my favourite hacks is to buy a big bag of croissants (especially if they're reduced to clear!), stuff them with ham, cheese and spinach and pop them in the freezer for a later date. It's quick, simple and perfect for hungry kids.

WHAT YOU NEED

- croissants
- baby spinach leaves
- shaved ham
- grated cheese
- foil

Slice open the croissants along the outside edge. I like to use a pair of scissors, as it makes the prep super fast, but just use a sharp knife if you prefer. Stuff the croissants with spinach leaves, ham and cheese, then wrap each one in a square of foil and place in the freezer for up to 1 month.

When it's time to eat, take a croissant out of the freezer and leave it to defrost for a little while you preheat the oven to 200°C. Place the croissant on a baking tray and pop it in the oven for 30–40 minutes or until the cheese has melted. Open up the foil and cook for a further 3–4 minutes to crisp up the croissant pastry (don't walk away and do something else as they can easily burn!).

Leave the croissants to cool a little, then fold back the foil and enjoy.

HINT

You can also heat these up in a sandwich press. If you do, remember to keep them in the foil to help them heat through and prevent them from burning.

I swear I'm not being lazy when I say this dish doesn't require exact quantities or a proper recipe! It all comes down to buying good-quality pork chops and adding a few key flavours, and you'll end up with a killer dish. I've had a go at writing this no-recipe recipe, but once you've made it a few times you won't even need it and will feel confident to add your own little twists.

Honey-mustard PORK CHOPS

Serves 4

1 rosemary sprig
1 tablespoon seeded mustard
huge dollop of dijon mustard
generous swirl of honey
2 garlic cloves, crushed
finely grated zest of 1 orange (do not add the juice – it will cure the pork and make it tough!)
4 good-sized pork chops
glug of olive oil

tip

Here are a few tips to take your pork chops from ordinary to extraordinary:

Make sure your chops are nice and thick, with a big, juicy piece of fat around the edge.

Be confident. Point to the one you want and ask your butcher to find three more exactly like it, so you're not adjusting the cooking time for different-sized chops. Don't be afraid to ask them to hold up different chops so you can see what's available.

Always bring the chops to room temperature before cooking - this helps them to cook more evenly.

Bruise the rosemary with your hands and tear it up a little, then throw it into a glass or ceramic bowl. Add the mustards, honey, garlic and orange zest and mix well. Add the pork chops and turn to coat in the marinade, then finish with a nice glug of olive oil to seal in all the goodness. Cover and marinate in the fridge for at least 1 hour or, better yet, overnight.

Take the chops out of the fridge an hour or so before you're ready to cook so they come to room temperature. Preheat the oven to 200°C.

Heat a large ovenproof frying pan over medium–high heat, add the chops and cook for 8–10 minutes or until they're really well browned on the base. Turn them over and whack the pan straight in the oven for another 8–10 minutes or until cooked the way you like them. Remember that honey can burn easily so keep an eye on the chops while they're cooking.

Take them out and let them rest for a good 5–10 minutes. This will make them nice and juicy. Team them with the zesty broccolini and slivered almonds on page 144 or any sides of your choice and you have got yourself one mean dinner!

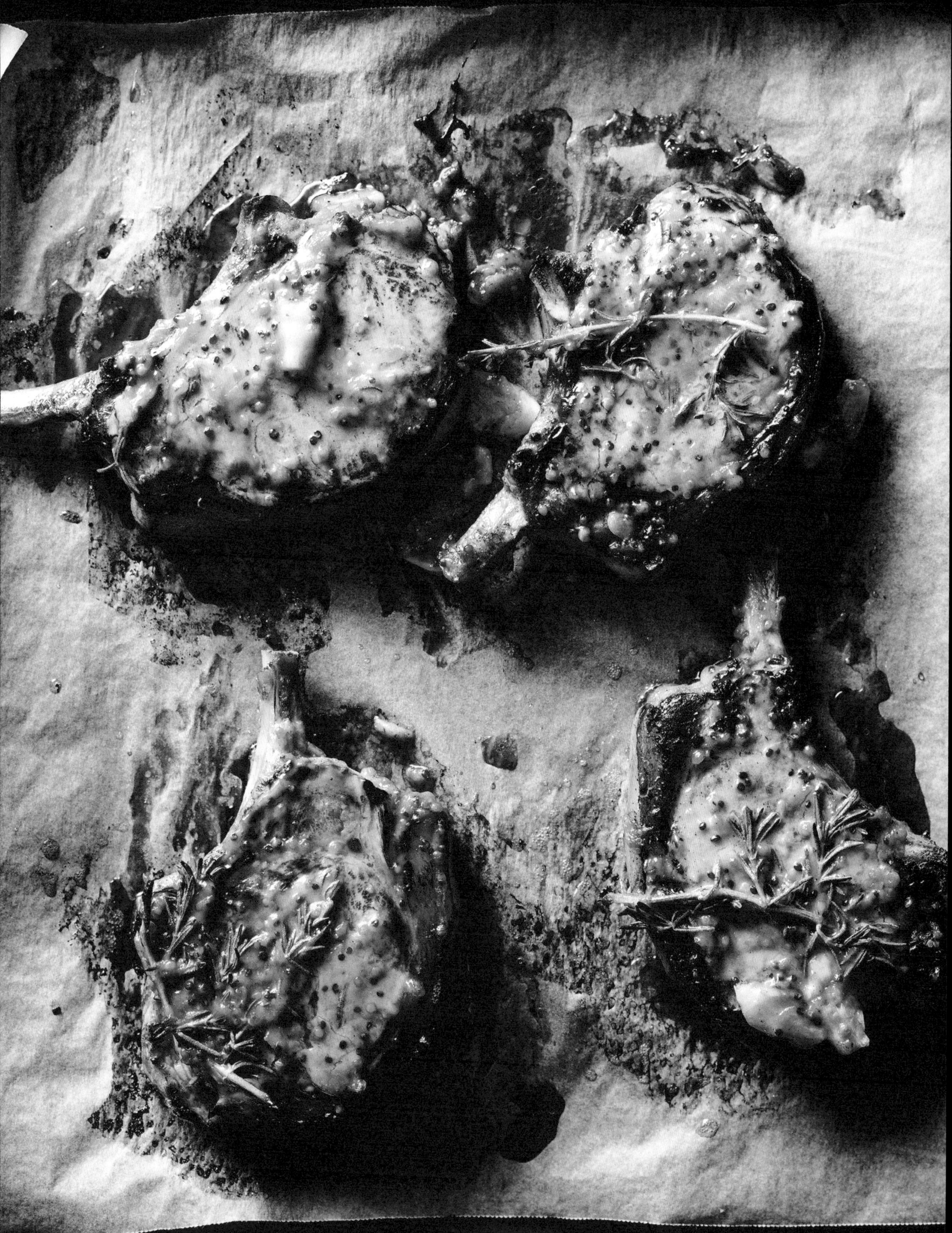

My baby sister is one of the quietest members of our family, but she's also the dark horse when it comes to cooking. We all talk a big game, but Sue-Lyn is the real deal. I think it's because she always cooks with love. She has a massive heart, and despite her tiny size she's also got a massive appetite! I love the way Sue-Lyn cooks and I'm so excited to share some of her recipes with you.

Her Italian meatballs are the best. I don't eat tomatoes so I usually eat these babies on their own, but obviously you need the passata to make the true Italian meatballs that everybody loves. Serve them with a salad or crusty baguettes so your guests can make their own meatball subs!

Sue-Lyn's Italian MEATBALLS

Serves 4

4 slices of white sandwich bread
milk, for soaking
500 g pork mince
3 teaspoons fennel seeds
1 onion, very finely chopped
1 egg, lightly beaten
finely grated zest of 1 lemon
3 tablespoons grated parmesan
sea salt and freshly ground black pepper
olive oil, for pan-frying
2 garlic cloves, finely chopped
700 g bottle tomato passata
1 tablespoon balsamic vinegar

FINISHING TOUCHES

100 g shaved parmesan
handful of flat-leaf parsley leaves, roughly chopped
finely grated zest of 1 lemon
lemon wedges
crusty baguette

tip

You can cook the meatballs the day before and keep them in the fridge overnight. Save the finishing touches until just before you're ready to serve.

If you're feeding a big tribe get some massive baguettes and baby rocket and make huge subs that can be cut into single-serve portions.

Put the bread slices in a shallow bowl and pour over enough milk to cover. Leave to soak for about 30 minutes.

Place the pork mince, fennel seeds, onion, egg, lemon zest, parmesan and some salt and pepper in a bowl.

One by one, grab your soaked slices of bread and give them a light squeeze first before adding them to the pork mixture. Using clean, wet hands, mush everything together, then shape into 12 large or 24 small meatballs. This might sound crazy, but if you slap each meatball against the inside of the bowl before rolling into its final shape, it will help get all the air out, giving you a meatier, juicier meatball.

Heat a splash of olive oil in a large frying pan over medium–high heat and cook the meatballs for 5–7 minutes or until sealed and nicely browned all over. Take them out of the pan with a slotted spoon and drain them on paper towel.

Add the garlic to the pan and pour in the passata and balsamic vinegar. Season with salt and pepper and simmer for 5 minutes. Return the meatballs to the pan and simmer for another 20 minutes or until cooked through.

Finish with a generous scattering of parmesan, parsley and lemon zest. Serve with some lemon wedges and crusty baguette. These meatballs are also great teamed with Italian coleslaw (see page 153).

This is one of the first recipes I ever shared on Facebook. A friend of mine left a comment saying that she'd never used raw snow peas in a dish before, and she wasn't sure how it would taste. I urged her to give it a try and she ended up loving the result. I was so happy for her, and it kick-started this whole journey of helping people to build confidence in the kitchen. She was unsure about trying something new, but she embraced my suggestions and still makes this for her family today!

MARINATED LAMB STEAKS *with* SOBA NOODLES, BROCCOLI *and* SNOW PEAS

Serves 4

4 x 100 g lamb steaks
270 g soba noodles
1 teaspoon vegetable oil
120 g (2 cups) broccoli florets
decent handful of snow peas, thinly sliced

MARINADE

1 teaspoon sambal oelek (chilli paste)
½ teaspoon sesame oil
2 tablespoons kecap manis
1 tablespoon soy sauce
1 heaped teaspoon honey
1 tablespoon chopped garlic chives (optional)

TO SERVE

sliced red chilli
sliced spring onion
sambal oelek (chilli paste)

To make the marinade, mix all the ingredients in a large glass or ceramic dish. Add the lamb steaks and turn to coat, then cover and place in the fridge to marinate – anything from 10 minutes to overnight is great.

Shortly before you are ready to cook the steaks, cook the soba noodles according to the packet instructions. Drain and set aside. Also, flick your kettle on so you have some boiling water on hand.

Heat the oil in a large frying pan over medium–high heat. Flash fry the steaks for about 3 minutes each side for medium, or until they are cooked the way you like them. Remove to a plate, cover with foil and rest. It's important to rest the lamb for at least half the time you cooked it – this allows all the fabulous juices to go back into the meat.

While the lamb is resting, throw the broccoli into the frying pan you cooked the lamb in and add 3 tablespoons of boiling water. Stir to deglaze the base of the pan, then braise the broccoli for about 4 minutes or until just tender. Add the cooked noodles and quickly toss to warm through.

Transfer the noodles to a serving plate and scatter the sliced snow peas over the top. Serve with the steaks and, if you like, some sliced chilli, spring onions and sambal oelek.

tip

If you want to make this vegetarian, just replace the lamb with a firm tofu and cook for the same amount of time.

This recipe is a great one to make ahead because it freezes really well. Buy a heap of chicken wings or a combination of wingettes and drumettes and marinate them all at once. Take what you need, then flash-freeze the rest on a lined baking tray (so they don't stick together). Once they're frozen solid, transfer to a freezer bag or airtight container. Now you've got a fantastic snack ready to go for parties. I love serving these chicken wings with a simple side of rice and fresh cucumber slices.

Honey soy-glazed CHICKEN WINGS

Serves 4

12 chicken wings or a mix of wingettes and drumettes
1 tablespoon sesame seeds
steamed rice and sliced cucumber, to serve

MARINADE

175 g (½ cup) runny honey
125 ml (½ cup) soy sauce
2 tablespoons kecap manis
2–3 garlic cloves, crushed
1 long red chilli, chopped (deseed if serving the kids)
3 cm piece of ginger, grated
¼ teaspoon freshly ground black pepper (optional)
1 teaspoon sesame oil

Preheat the oven to 180°C and line a large baking tray with baking paper.

To make the marinade, mix all the ingredients in a large bowl.

Now add the chicken wings and toss to coat in the marinade. Cover and leave to marinate in the fridge for at least 1 hour or overnight. (You can even pop it all into a zip-lock bag and freeze for a ready-prepped meal another time.)

Tip the marinated wings onto the prepared tray in a single layer and slide into the oven. Bake for 20 minutes, then reduce the temperature to 160°C and bake for another 40 minutes.

Take the wings out of the oven and sprinkle with the sesame seeds. Leave to rest for 10 minutes so they are nice and juicy.

Serve with steamed rice and fresh cucumber.

EMMYLOU'S LIFE HACKS

MIDWEEK SWEET POTATOES

This is my perfect midweek dinner hack for when I don't have much time to spend in the kitchen. Sweet potatoes are nutritious and filling, plus you can mix and match the toppings to use whatever you have in the fridge.

Preheat the oven to 180°C. Place similar-sized sweet potatoes on a baking tray. Rub them all over with a little coconut or olive oil and a nice pinch of salt and whack them in the oven for 1 hour or until cooked through and crispy on the outside.

Once your sweet potatoes are beautifully roasted and the flesh is tender, use a pair of kitchen scissors to slice them open lengthways (be careful as they'll be bloody hot!) and gently prise them open.

Grab a handful of baby spinach and, using your scissors, snip and press the spinach into the flesh of the sweet potato. This helps wilt down the spinach to make room for your other ingredients. Use your scissors to snip and mix the other ingredients into the potato before topping with sour cream or whatever takes your fancy.

Some of my favourite topping ingredients include:

- Grated cheese
- Baby spinach leaves
- Canned corn
- Sour cream
- Pickled jalapenos
- Baked beans
- Leftover pulled pork (see page 114) or bolognese

Once again, my Insta tribe has spoken and these rissoles have become a massive hit all around Australia. They're a great midweek meal, and a clever way to sneak a few veggies in for the kids. I love popping them into lunchboxes and they're really popular at parties. Beef and apple sounds like a strange combo, but trust me when I say the kids will devour these little beauties.

BEEF *and* APPLE RISSOLES

Makes 12

500 g lean beef mince
1 red apple, cored and grated
1 onion, finely chopped
1 garlic clove, crushed
1 carrot, grated
1 egg
sea salt and freshly ground black pepper
breadcrumbs, for coating
vegetable oil, for pan-frying
your favourite salad leaves, to serve
lemon wedges, to serve

Mix the mince, apple, onion, garlic and carrot in a bowl. Crack in the egg and mix well until combined. Season with salt and pepper.

With wet hands, form the mixture into six rissoles. This might sound crazy, but if you slap each rissole against the inside of the bowl before rolling into its final shape, it will help get all the air out, giving you a meatier, juicier rissole. Toss the rissoles in breadcrumbs until evenly coated.

Heat a splash of oil in a large frying pan over medium heat. Add the rissoles and cook for about 10 minutes on each side or until beautifully golden and cooked through. Season with a little extra salt.

Serve with some fresh green leaves and a squeeze of lemon. They're also great with mashed veggies or just on their own as a snack.

If you were at my 30th birthday party, there are two things you'll remember. The first is probably the giant video projection of me skydiving naked. The second is my brother Kim-Lee's mini chicken schnitzels. I've never seen people demolish party food more quickly in my life. In fact, I vividly remember watching two of my friends fight over the last one. Typical ... Kim-Lee is the only sibling who would have the balls to upstage me at my own party!

Kim-Lee's CHICKEN SCHNITZELS

Serves 8

4 large chicken breast fillets
300 g (2 cups) plain flour
sea salt and freshly ground black pepper
3 eggs, lightly beaten
2½ tablespoons milk
180 g (3 cups) panko breadcrumbs
vegetable oil, for frying
lemon wedges, to serve
aioli, to serve (optional)

Slice each chicken breast in half horizontally so you have eight thin fillets. Working with one fillet at a time, place the fillet between two sheets of plastic wrap and use a meat mallet or rolling pin to flatten the chicken until it's roughly 5 mm thick.

Set up a mixing station with three shallow bowls: one for the flour seasoned with salt and pepper, one for the beaten egg and milk, and one for the breadcrumbs.

Working with one piece of chicken at a time, coat it in the flour, then the egg and milk and finally the breadcrumbs, making sure the crumbs completely coat the chicken. Place in the fridge for 1 hour to firm up.

Pour enough vegetable oil into a large frying pan to reach a depth of 1 cm and place over medium heat. Working in batches so you don't overcrowd the pan, fry the schnitzels for 2–3 minutes on each side or until cooked through and golden brown. Drain on paper towel.

Season with salt flakes, squeeze over some lemon juice and serve with aioli for dipping, if you like.

tip

If you like the idea of a beef schnitzel, use a tender cut, such as eye fillet.

Top the chicken with prosciutto, tomato sauce and mozzarella and put it under the grill until golden for a quick chicken parmigiana.

When it comes to the real queen of our family, my big sister Treena will always wear the crown. Although, it would probably be made out of daisies instead of jewels because she is a total earth mother. Treena is all about home grown, and she makes the most incredible meals with produce from her own garden. This salt and pepper fish is such a riot of flavour and is perfect served with my Vietnamese salad on page 161 or the Italian coleslaw on page 153.

Salt and pepper FISH

Serves 6–8

1 kg skinless firm white fish fillets, cut into 3–4 cm pieces (see tip)
125 ml (½ cup) vegetable oil
3 tablespoons oyster sauce, to serve

SEASONED FLOUR
90 g (¾ cup) plain flour
1 teaspoon sea salt
2½ teaspoons freshly ground black pepper

DRESSING
1 teaspoon olive oil
2 spring onions, thinly sliced
2 long red chillies, deseeded, thinly sliced
2.5 cm piece of ginger, julienned

To make the seasoned flour, combine all the ingredients in a shallow bowl. Add the fish and toss to coat, shaking off any excess flour.

Heat the oil in a large frying pan over medium heat. You will know the oil is ready if you put the end of a wooden spoon into the oil and bubbles start to appear. Shallow-fry the fish for 3–4 minutes each side or until lovely and golden. Remove with a slotted spoon and drain on a plate lined with paper towel.

To make the dressing, heat the olive oil in a small frying pan over medium heat. Add the spring onion, chilli and ginger and gently cook for 2 minutes or until warmed through.

Place the salt and pepper fish on a serving plate. Drizzle over the oyster sauce and the dressing, sprinkle over a little more salt and serve immediately.

tip

You can use any white fish you like, but I usually choose groper or snapper.

THERMOS HOT DOGS

Hot dogs in a thermos – genius! These bad boys are perfect to take to the footy or a picnic at the beach. Kids and grown-ups love them and you can mix and match the condiments so everyone can make their own perfect dawg. Here's what you do:

Warm your thermos by filling it with boiling water. Set aside while you prepare your hot dogs.

Place your hot dogs in a saucepan of water and bring to the boil for 30 seconds (you don't want them to boil for too long or they'll split).

Meanwhile, boil another kettle of water.

Now that your hot dogs are ready, tip out the boiling water from your thermos and, using tongs, place as many hot dogs as you can fit into your thermos. Top up the thermos with boiling water and close the lid.

Don't forget to pack some buttered hot dog rolls and any condiments that you like and you're good to go!

If you have a good-quality thermos, these will stay hot all day.

COMFORT FOOD

Pastas and bakes for cosy times

My gorgeous friend Brad Johnson owns Canteen, a cafe in the South Melbourne Market, and he makes the most incredible, rustic, home-style foods. These make the perfect addition to a breakfast, brunch or even lunch setting. I also love to put them on a grazing table for something different.

If you'd like to make a vegetarian version simply swap the bacon for ribbons of zucchini. You will need a 6-hole silicone muffin tray for this recipe.

Brad's BREAKFAST CUPS

Makes 6

6 streaky bacon rashers (or use ribbons of zucchini for a vegetarian version)
small handful of baby spinach leaves
12 eggs
sea salt and freshly ground black pepper
chopped flat-leaf parsley leaves, for sprinkling
snow pea sprouts, to serve (optional)

Preheat the oven to 180°C.

Place the silicone muffin tray on a baking tray (this will make it easy for you to transport it in and out of the oven). Line each muffin hole with a rasher of streaky bacon or a few zucchini ribbons and arrange 3–4 spinach leaves on top.

Carefully crack two eggs into each hole, season with salt and pepper and sprinkle over a little parsley.

Bake for 20 minutes and boom! You have the most perfect breakfast, snack or lunchbox addition. You could even serve a couple of these with a salad for dinner! And if you want them to look even prettier when serving, top with some snow pea sprouts.

tip

You need to crack a lot of eggs to make these breakfast cups, so chances are you'll have a stray piece of shell that gets stuck in the egg – especially if the kids help you! Instead of messing about trying to remove the shell with your fingers or a spoon, simply use one of the big pieces of shell to fish out the unwanted fragment – the sharp side of the shell easily cuts through the whites and you'll get the job done much more quickly and easily.

LOVE

I've always loved a good afternoon tea, especially when I was working in a 9–5 job. And nobody appreciated a good arvo tea like the ladies at Endeavour Hills Pharmacy! I got a job there when I first moved to Melbourne, and I was the youngest person on the team. We would take it in turns to bake afternoon tea and I would entertain everyone with my crazy skydiving stories. One day I mentioned that I had never tasted pumpkin soup, and I swear they nearly fainted. Once everyone had recovered from the shock, I was given about five different recipes on the spot. I spent ages creating my perfect pumpkin soup and finally struck gold when I began to slow roast the pumpkin beforehand. I've been making it this way ever since.

The perfect slow-roasted PUMPKIN SOUP

Serves 6

- 1 butternut pumpkin, halved lengthways, seeds removed
- melted coconut oil, for roasting and drizzling
- 1 head of garlic, unpeeled
- 1 onion, unpeeled
- 1 sweet potato
- 2 celery sticks, diced
- 2 carrots, diced
- ½ teaspoon curry powder
- 1 teaspoon sweet paprika
- 1.5 litres vegetable stock
- ½ teaspoon ground or freshly grated nutmeg
- sea salt and freshly ground black pepper
- crusty bread and butter, to serve

tip

This soup freezes beautifully. Just let it cool, then pour it into airtight containers and whack it in the freezer for up to 3 months.

Preheat the oven to 160°C and line a large roasting tin with baking paper.

Rub the pumpkin with oil and pop it, cut side down, in the prepared tin. Drizzle a little oil over the garlic then lift up one pumpkin half, place the garlic in the hollow and replace the pumpkin, cut-side down, on the tray. This will protect the garlic so it can gently roast without burning, making the flesh mild and sweet.

Add the onion and sweet potato to the tin and rub with oil. Now pop it all in the oven to slow roast for about 1 hour.

Heat a splash of oil in a large heavy-based saucepan over medium heat. Add the celery, carrot, curry powder and paprika and cook, stirring, for 4 minutes or until softened.

Using a spoon, scoop out the pumpkin flesh and add it to the carrot and celery. Peel the skin off the onion. Roughly chop the onion and sweet potato and add them to the pan. Finally, squeeze the flesh from the garlic into the pan.

Pour in 1 litre of the stock, give it a good stir and let it come to a simmer. At this stage you can add the rest of the stock, but you may also like to wait to see how thick the soup is after blending. Sprinkle in the nutmeg. Simmer for about 10 minutes or until everything is lovely and soft, then blend with a stick blender until smooth. Make sure you keep the blender submerged in the soup so it doesn't splatter everywhere.

Transfer to serving bowls, season with salt and pepper and drizzle with a little melted coconut oil. Serve with crusty bread and butter.

I've included my big brother Khanh's omelette recipe in this book because he would kick my arse if I left it out! This is my favourite kind of comfort food – super simple to prep, but full of flavour and warmth.

My big brother Khanh's PORK *and* CABBAGE OMELETTE

Serves 4

1 tablespoon vegetable or olive oil
500 g pork mince
250 g (about 3 heaped cups) shredded white cabbage
5 garlic cloves, crushed
2 long red chillies, deseeded and finely chopped
1 teaspoon kecap manis
1½ teaspoons fish sauce
1 teaspoon brown sugar
3 eggs

TO SERVE
steamed rice
sliced cucumber
chilli sambal

Heat the oil in a large frying pan over medium heat, add the pork mince and cook for 4–5 minutes or until nicely browned, breaking up any large lumps with a wooden spoon. Tip the mince into a colander and drain.

While the pork is draining, add the cabbage and garlic to the pan and cook for 2–3 minutes or until the cabbage starts to wilt. Return the mince to the pan and add the chilli, kecap manis, fish sauce and brown sugar and cook, tossing, for a further 2 minutes.

Crack the eggs into the pan, giving each one a quick stir to loosely mix the egg through the pork mixture. Gently flatten the mixture onto the base of the pan, then reduce the heat to medium–low and cook for a further 2 minutes or until the egg is cooked.

Serve with steamed rice, fresh cucumber and your favourite chilli sambal on the side.

I've been making this pasta since my skydiving days in Barwon Heads on Victoria's Bellarine Peninsula. After every session, I would get everyone to chuck in a few bucks and send them back to my place. I would go and buy the ingredients, then come home and cook up a massive feast. The combo of prawns and chorizo not only tastes divine, but it's a great way to feed lots of people without blowing your entire budget on seafood.

CHORIZO *and* PRAWN PASTA

Serves 4

500 g packet thin spaghetti
2 raw chorizo sausages, chopped
1 long red chilli, finely chopped (if you don't like it spicy, remove the seeds)
12 large raw prawns, peeled and deveined
4 garlic cloves, crushed
1 lemon
2 large handfuls of rocket leaves
extra-virgin olive oil, for drizzling
grated parmesan, to serve

Throw the spaghetti into a large saucepan of salted boiling water and cook to al dente according to the packet instructions.

Meanwhile, heat a large frying pan over medium heat. Place the chorizo and chilli in the pan and cook for 5–7 minutes to release all the oils and flavours of the sausage. Add the prawns and cook for 1–2 minutes max – they should just be starting to change colour.

By now the spaghetti should be very close to al dente.

Add the garlic to the pan and let it cook for 30 seconds. Use a pair of tongs to grab the spaghetti out of the water and plonk it into the hot chorizo pan. Yes, you can drain the pasta if you like, but I find that once you have got the hang of this method it all just flows, and transferring it straight from the pan of water means you get a little liquid in there as well, which helps create a sauce.

Zest the lemon and add to the pan, along with the rocket. Cut the lemon in half and squeeze in a bit of lemon juice. Drizzle in a glug of olive oil and give it one more toss.

Finish with a good sprinkling of parmesan and get ready to chow down. Cut the remaining lemon half into wedges and serve alongside.

This simple and comforting dish uses glutinous rice, which becomes really sticky and delicious when cooked. Meanwhile, the tofu steaks are coated in the same style of marinade that I use for the pork skewers on page 120. I just add some chilli and swap the fish sauce for kecap manis, which is an Indonesian sweet soy sauce. The trick here is to cut your slabs of tofu quite thickly - that way they have a soft centre rather than going all leathery. You'll need to start this recipe the day before to soak your rice.

CHARGRILLED TOFU STEAKS *with* THAI STICKY RICE

Serves 4

500 g (2½ cups) glutinous rice (see tip)
500 g firm tofu, cut into thick slices

MARINADE
6 garlic cloves, peeled
1 lemongrass stalk, white part only, finely chopped
1 bird's eye chilli
pinch of sea salt
1 tablespoon grated palm sugar
3 tablespoons coconut milk
2 tablespoons kecap manis
1 tablespoon light soy sauce
1 tablespoon finely chopped coriander stalks
2 teaspoons vegetable oil

TO SERVE
lime wedges
tomato wedges
Thai basil sprigs

tip

Glutinous rice is available from supermarkets and Asian grocers. Traditionally, a Thai bamboo cone basket is used to steam it - you can find these at most Asian grocers.

It is possible to make this without soaking the rice first, but it will take a lot longer to cook ... like 2 hours! You will have to keep checking the water level too, so it's best to soak overnight if you can.

Soak the rice in water overnight.

To make the marinade, place the garlic, lemongrass, chilli and salt in a mortar and pound with a pestle to create a paste. Combine with the remaining ingredients in a bowl.

Place the tofu in a glass or ceramic dish, pour over the marinade and turn to coat. Cover and place in the fridge to marinate for at least couple of hours or, better still, overnight.

The next day, add water to a large saucepan until it's about one-quarter full. This is important – you don't want the water touching the cone basket. Bring the water to a gentle simmer.

Drain the rice and place it in a Thai bamboo basket (see tip). Set the basket over the pan of water and cover the rice with a piece of muslin or baking paper, then find a random saucepan lid from your kitchen (don't worry there is always one that fits) and create a seal. Simmer over medium–low heat for 15–20 minutes or until the rice is tender (the water may need to be topped up during cooking).

Give the rice a little fluff with a fork and transfer it to your serving dish or a traditional bamboo sticky rice container. Fluffing it will prevent it from going hard and crusty. Sticky rice does not have to be served piping hot so it is something you can make earlier if you like.

To cook the tofu steaks, heat a chargrill pan over medium–high heat or a barbecue grill plate to medium–hot. Grill the tofu steaks for 5 minutes on each side or until nicely charred.

Transfer the tofu steaks to a serving platter and add the lime, tomato wedges and Thai basil sprigs. Serve with a big spoonful of sticky rice.

If there's one thing that can help heal a broken heart, it's food. In my late 20s I split up with a guy who I thought was 'the one'. I was taking it really hard, and one day I received a text from a girlfriend I hadn't seen in ages. It simply said, 'Hey Lou, I just made a lasagne and thought I would bring it over tonight with a bottle of wine.' We ate, I cried, we laughed and something inside me began to heal. I'll never forget that simple act of kindness, and since then I've always made this lasagne for friends when they're having a rough time. It took me ages to perfect this recipe because I could never get the quantities right. I'd have too much meat, or not enough sauce or I'd run out of lasagne sheets halfway through. Save yourself the drama and follow these steps for a foolproof lasagne that could feed an army. Alternatively, divide it up into smaller portions and freeze. Or take it to a friend's house with a bottle of wine and indulge in the ultimate comfort food together.

Foolproof FAMILY LASAGNE

Serves 8

1 tablespoon olive oil
1 large onion, finely chopped
1 celery stalk, finely chopped
1 large carrot, grated
3 garlic cloves, crushed
1 kg beef mince
500 g jar bolognese sauce
700 g bottle tomato passata
375 g dried lasagne sheets
500 g grated pizza cheese
100 g sharp parmesan, grated
sea salt and freshly ground black pepper

BECHAMEL

100 g butter
75 g (½ cup) plain flour
1.25 litres full-cream milk
½ teaspoon ground nutmeg
sea salt

tip

To make the bechamel gluten free, use potato flour instead of plain flour.

You can easily bulk out this lasagne with extra veggies; just add a layer of baby spinach or thinly sliced mushroom on top of the first and second layers of bechamel.

Heat the olive oil in a large, deep frying pan over medium heat. Add the onion, celery and carrot and sauté for 5–7 minutes, then add the garlic and sauté for 2 minutes. Add the mince, breaking up any lumps with the back of a wooden spoon, and cook for 7 minutes or until browned. Drain away any excess liquid in the pan, then add the bolognese sauce and passata. Simmer, stirring occasionally, for 10 minutes.

Preheat the oven to 180°C.

To make the bechamel, melt the butter in a saucepan over medium–high heat, throw in the flour and whisk immediately to make sure there are no lumps. Cook for a couple of minutes to cook out the flour flavour, then gradually add the milk, whisking constantly to form a smooth sauce. Switch over to a wooden spoon and stir over medium–low heat for 10–15 minutes or until the sauce is thick enough to coat the back of the spoon. Add the nutmeg and season to taste with salt.

Now it's time to layer your lasagne. Start with a small smear of the bolognese on the bottom of a 20 x 30 cm baking dish (or similar – don't worry if your dish doesn't match these measurements exactly) then add a layer of lasagne sheets. Sprinkle over some of the grated pizza blend cheese, then add a layer of bolognese and a layer of bechamel.

Repeat the layering. After a couple of layers, give your lasagne sheets a little push – this will weigh them down a bit and help give an even finish.

Finish the layering with lasagne sheets and the last of the bechamel. Cover the dish with baking paper and then foil and bake for 45 minutes.

Take off the baking paper and foil and sprinkle over the parmesan. Return to the oven for a further 15 minutes or until the cheese is melted and golden. Let the lasagne sit for a few minutes and season with extra salt and pepper before serving.

LOS ANGELES SURF CLUB
LA
SURF CLUB

This dish is a big, hearty bastard that basically takes care of itself. Once you've chopped the onions it can all sit in the slow cooker or a casserole dish and bubble away until the meat falls apart. I use beef cheeks but you can easily substitute it with oyster blade steak. I love that you can make this ahead of time and it tastes even better the next day. This dish also freezes really well. Serve it with polenta, mash or rice and plenty of veggies for the kids.

BEEF CHEEKS IN RED WINE *with creamy polenta*

Serves 6–8

olive oil, for pan-frying
1.5 kg beef cheeks (or you could use oyster blade), cut into large chunks
2 onions, thinly sliced
1 teaspoon ground cumin
1 tablespoon sweet paprika
4 thyme sprigs
6 garlic cloves, crushed
1 tablespoon red wine vinegar
400 g can whole tomatoes
375 ml (1½ cups) red wine
finely chopped flat-leaf parsley leaves, to serve

CREAMY POLENTA

150 g (1 cup) fine polenta
100 ml pouring cream (full-cream milk is also fine)
3 tablespoons finely grated parmesan, plus extra to serve
40 g butter
sea salt, to taste

tip

Pour any leftover polenta into a lined baking tray, let it set in the fridge and then cut into polenta chips. Shallow-fry in 60 ml (¼ cup) of olive oil over medium heat until golden on both sides. They are delicious served with aioli or even pesto!

You can cook these beef cheeks in either a casserole dish or a slow cooker. If using a casserole dish, preheat the oven to 170°C.

Heat a splash of olive oil in a heavy-based frying pan over medium–high heat, add the beef in small batches and cook until browned and sealed. Transfer to your slow cooker or casserole dish.

Reduce the heat to medium, add another 2 tablespoons of olive oil to the pan and throw in the onion. Cook, stirring occasionally, for about 10 minutes to really get it caramelised. Now add the cumin, paprika, thyme, garlic, vinegar, tomatoes and wine. Bring to a simmer, then transfer to the slow cooker or casserole dish and stir well.

If using a slow cooker, cover with the lid and cook on medium heat for 3–4 hours until the meat is beautifully tender. If using a casserole dish, cover with the lid and pop in the oven for 1–1½ hours.

Once the beef is ready, make sure you have all the polenta ingredients measured and ready to go. Oh, and you will need a whisk!

Pour 750 ml (3 cups) of water into a heavy-based saucepan and bring to a rolling boil over high heat. With a whisk in one hand, add the polenta in a slow, steady stream, making sure you whisk constantly. Reduce the heat to low and replace the whisk with a wooden spoon. Simmer, stirring constantly, for 10 minutes or until the polenta has thickened and become nice and soft. Remove from the heat and stir in the remaining ingredients. Mix until combined, then taste and add a little more salt if needed.

To serve, spoon a dollop of polenta onto each plate, top with the beef cheeks and sprinkle over some parsley and extra parmesan.

My kids don't dig this creamy pasta, which is weird and frankly annoying. Adults love it, so I save this for big dinner parties where it goes brilliantly with a few glasses of wine. I always serve this pasta with a little salad made up of bitter leaves (radicchio is good) and balsamic vinegar to cut through the heaviness of the gorgonzola. Try to find bowtie pasta (farfalle) if you can. The little creases soak up the sauce and I love that you can stab your fork in and get a bit of everything at the same time.

GORGONZOLA *and* SPECK BOWTIES

Serves 4–6

500 g bowtie pasta (farfalle)
olive oil, for cooking
sea salt
250 g piece of speck, cut into 1 cm cubes
155 g (1 cup) frozen or fresh peas
1 garlic clove, crushed (optional)
125–250 ml (½–1 cup) double cream
100 g gorgonzola
grated parmesan, to taste
coarsely ground black pepper

Bring a large saucepan of water to the boil over high heat. Throw in the pasta, along with a splash of olive oil and a good pinch of salt, then cook according to the packet instructions until al dente.

Meanwhile, heat a good glug of olive oil in a large heavy-based frying pan over medium heat, add the speck and cook until it starts to get a little crispy. Whack in the peas and add the garlic (if using).

Pour in 125 ml (½ cup) of cream and give it a good stir, then add the rest of the cream if you want lots of sauce. Crumble in the gorgonzola and simmer for a couple of minutes or until the gorgonzola melts into the sauce. Stir in a really heavy-handed grating of parmesan and turn off the heat.

Drain the bowties and toss them through the sauce.

Divide the pasta among shallow bowls and finish off with salt, pepper and a bit more parmesan. Serve alongside a gorgeous salad of bitter leaves tossed with a balsamic dressing, if you like.

'If there's one thing that can heal a broken heart, it's food.'

Who doesn't love mac and cheese? This is comfort food at its best. If I'm serving this to the kids I'll throw in some frozen peas and corn or blanched broccoli. It's cheap, easy and is great on its own or served alongside sausages, chicken wings or whatever you've got. Hell, chuck it in a toastie for all I care! If you want to get fancy, try using gruyere cheese instead of parmesan.

MAC AND CHEESE
to make everyone happy

Serves 6

500 g macaroni (or any short pasta shape really)
50 g butter
2 tablespoons plain flour
500 ml (2 cups) milk
1 tablespoon dijon mustard
150 g (1 cup) mixed frozen peas and corn, thawed and drained
185 g (1½ cups) grated pizza cheese
50 g grated parmesan (for something more decadent, a big handful of gruyere is amazing), plus extra for sprinkling
sea salt
fresh breadcrumbs, for sprinkling

Preheat the oven to 180°C.

Cook the pasta according to the packet instructions, then drain.

Meanwhile, melt the butter in a large heavy-based saucepan over medium heat and let it bubble away for a minute or so. Grab a whisk, sprinkle in the flour and cook, whisking constantly, for about 2 minutes or until it starts to get a bit frothy.

Still whisking, slowly pour in the milk, then gently stir as it starts to thicken. Whisk in the mustard.

Swap the whisk for a nice big serving spoon and stir in your macaroni, peas and corn. Throw in the grated cheeses and mix while it gets all stringy and gooey. Season with salt to taste.

Pour into a large baking dish and finish with a good layer of grated parmesan and breadcrumbs. Bake for 20 minutes or until golden.

Allow to cool slightly before serving.

ENTERTAINING

Wow your guests without breaking a sweat!

Menu plans

When I've got family or friends coming around, I like to plan ahead as much as possible so I don't have to spend all my time in the kitchen once they arrive. So, to help get myself organised, I like to write menu plans to work out exactly what I am going to make. That way I can see if I've got too many complicated dishes on the go and need to swap one or two for something more simple. It also allows me to check that I've got a good range of flavours going on and that nothing is going to clash. Here are some of my favourite menu plans based on the recipes you'll find in this book!

THE PERFECT SUNDAY ROAST

Crank up the oven and get ready to wow your guests with this decadent and delicious Sunday roast. When I'm planning a meal, I like to feature the same ingredient across a number of dishes, and in this menu you'll notice lots of orange and citrus flavours coming through.

* Porchetta with perfect pork crackle (see page 130)
* Best ever roast spuds (see page 138)
* Colin Fassnidge's whole roast pumpkin (see page 154)
* Apple and fennel slaw (see page 158)
* Brandied oranges with whipped cream (see page 169)

GIRLS' NIGHT IN

This is the perfect menu for when your girlfriends come over. The pasta is really rich, so I always serve it with lovely, crisp broccolini to add some freshness.

* Chorizo and prawn pasta (see page 52)
* Zesty broccolini with slivered almonds (see page 144)
* Chocolate cheesecake brownies (see page 191)

WINTER GRAZING TABLE

Adding a few warm dishes is a great way to turn my summer grazing table (see page 76) into an incredibly festive winter spread. You don't need to make all of these dishes, simply choose two or three and pop them down on the grazing table just before your guests arrive.

* Pulled pork with smoky barbecue sauce (see page 114)
* Warm roasted cauliflower dip (see page 86)
* Cheese and spinach cobb loaf (see page 88)
* Crumbed parsnip chips (see page 143)
* Chocolate brownies with drunken cherries (see page 184)

THAI BANQUET

This simple and delicious Thai banquet is such an easy way to impress friends or family when they come over for dinner – and kids will love the pork skewers and sticky rice!

* Spicy som tum (see page 148)
* Moo ping pork skewers (see page 120)
* Chargrilled tofu steaks (see page 57)
* Thai sticky rice (see page 57)

MOVIE NIGHT

Who wants to mess around with cutlery when it's movie night? All you need to serve these dishes are some napkins and your hands. Hit pause to run and get the ice cream sandwiches out of the freezer for dessert – I guarantee you'll have some very happy guests!

* Honey soy-glazed chicken wings (see page 33)
* Pork spring rolls (see page 108)
* The party pizza (see page 124)
* Ice cream sandwiches (see page 175)

VEGAN BANQUET

More and more people are going vegan or reducing the amount of meat they eat, so having a delicious vegan spread like this up your sleeve is really handy. Get confident cooking these recipes and your vegan friends will be inviting themselves over every weekend.

* Colin Fassnidge's whole roast pumpkin (see page 154)
* Freekeh salad with cranberry dressing (see page 136) – replace the butter with olive oil and simply leave out the cheese
* Orange, spinach and cranberry salad (see page 147)
* Vegan apple and berry crumble (see page 171)

PARTY

Whether you are hosting a kids' party, 40th birthday, Mother's Day lunch or Christmas gathering, this menu will get you through in style!

* Sausage rolls – go for the pork and fennel sausage rolls (see page 16) if you're feeding kids or the Middle Eastern sausage rolls (see page 85) if you're catering for adults
* Kim-Lee's chicken schnitzels (see page 39) – you can make mini schnitzels or do regular-sized ones and simply slice them up so that they are easy to eat as finger food. Serve with my stick-blender mayo (see page 162)
* The party pizza (see page 124)
* Chocolate cheesecake brownies (see page 191)
* Unbelievably dreamy rocky road (see page 200)
* Chaja mess (see page 179)

FEEDING THE TRIBE

Often when we invite a heap of people over, we get caught up in making lots of different dishes. My advice is to keep it simple – focus on a small number of dishes that can feed a crowd and ensure you spend minimal time in the kitchen. This menu is so easy – once you get the shoulder of lamb into the oven all you need to do is make a big bowl of salad and pick up some bread and dips from the shops!

* Slow-roasted lamb shoulder (see page 92)
* Pickled red onion (see page 92)
* My sister's Italian coleslaw (see page 153)
* Good-quality souvlaki bread
* Store-bought dips, such as tzatziki

Summer GRAZING TABLE

A grazing table represents everything I love about entertaining. It's generous, it brings people together, it's gorgeous to look at and is usually one of the most talked-about parts of the event. You could say a grazing table is a visual representation of how I see myself as a host!

This particular section of the book is very close to my heart. When I was trying to get my presenting career off the ground I would create grazing tables as a way to earn money. It was a steep learning curve, and I very quickly understood the importance of preparation, budgeting, problem solving and thinking on my feet.

I love the interactive nature of a grazing table. You can position it in the middle of the room for a 360-degree experience or scatter a few smaller grazing tables around the room to create pockets of activity. They can be chic and elegant, earthy and rustic, or funky and mismatched depending on the types of platters you use.

When it comes to putting together a grazing table, timing is everything. You need to begin planning a few weeks in advance. Head to your favourite op-shops and look for gorgeous plates, bowls, saucers and platters. You might want to stick to a theme (e.g. all white) or embrace the mismatched look. To up the ante, look for cake stands, wooden boxes or wooden boards with legs to add height to your grazing table – this allows you to showcase particular ingredients in a spectacular way.

When I first started out, I would sit down with a pencil and paper and map the whole table out. I would draw a diagram of where everything should go so I didn't get flustered on the day. I would put sticky notes on each bowl, plate or platter with its ingredient clearly labelled. This is actually really handy if your guests arrive early and want to help. You can simply point them towards the pre-labelled dishes and away they go. Make life easy by prepping your ingredients the night before. Wash and chop the fruit, pre-roll your deli meats, roast the veggies for your dips and put your pulled pork on to cook if you are including that on your table.

A grazing table is the perfect way to showcase seasonal produce. In winter embrace berries, nuts and warm dips, while in summer it's all about bright pops of colour thanks to tropical fruits and fresh flowers.

The best part about a grazing table is that it can be adapted to suit any budget. You can go all out and purchase five incredible cheeses from a specialty deli, or focus on one show-stopping cheese as your centrepiece. Sometimes I might invest in an expensive leg of ham but use cheap antipasto ingredients from my local supermarket. You can make your own dips, or use store bought and pop them into little bowls drizzled with olive oil and sprinkled with paprika or some fresh chives. Olives are an inexpensive way to bulk out your table, as are pretzels, nuts and dried fruit. Look for what's on special, what's in season and raid your garden (or your neighbour's!) for fresh foliage, herbs and flowers to make the whole thing pop.

HOW TO BUILD A KILLER GRAZING TABLE

Here are some of my favourite grazing table elements. Not all of the items listed are pictured and you definitely do not need to buy everything I've suggested. Pick and choose based on how many guests you are feeding as well as the size of your table and budget.

Bread and crackers

- Turkish bread, lightly toasted
- Sesame wheat crackers
- Bread sticks
- Lavosh
- Sliced sourdough
- Pita chips
- Pretzels

Meats

- Chorizo
- Sliced salami
- Leg of ham
- Prosciutto
- Pulled pork (see page 114)

Antipasto

- Olives
- Semi-dried tomatoes
- Cornichons
- Pickled onions

Fruit and sweets

- Assorted dried fruit and nuts
- Dried orange rings
- Fresh or dried figs
- Grapes
- Strawberries, blueberries and mulberries
- Pomegranate
- Quince paste
- Dark chocolate
- Chocolate brownies with drunken cherries (see page 184)

Dips

- Hummus
- Warm roasted cauliflower dip (see page 86)
- Spicy capsicum dip

Cheese

- Wheel of brie (top it with some fresh honeycomb and edible flowers for extra va va voom!)
- Cheddar
- Blue cheese
- Log of feta
- Bocconcini (they look great threaded onto skewers with cherry tomatoes and basil or other herbs)

Vegetables

- Orange, spinach and cranberry salad (see page 147)
- Vine or cherry tomatoes
- Crumbed parsnip chips (see page 143)

Decorations

- Whole large fruits – I love using pineapple and papaya to add height and colour to the table
- Gum leaves or other foliage, such as passionfruit or grape vine leaves
- Flowers
- Nuts in their shells

These sausage rolls are spicy little mofos, so if you're not really into a lot of spice, either halve the quantity of harissa or leave it out altogether. They are brilliant for relaxed entertaining and come together incredibly quickly. This mixture makes a lot – 72 sausage rolls to be precise! So, if you're short on time, halve the ingredients and make 36 or use the remaining mixture to make mini meatballs (see tip).

Middle Eastern SAUSAGE ROLLS

Makes 72

1 kg lamb mince
1 onion, finely grated
2 garlic cloves, crushed
2–3 tablespoons harissa, or to taste
60 g (⅓ cup) dried apricots, finely chopped
60 g (½ cup) slivered almonds
large handful of coriander leaves, finely chopped
2 teaspoons ground cumin
2 teaspoons ground coriander
½ teaspoon ground ginger
sea salt and freshly ground black pepper
6 frozen puff pastry sheets, slightly thawed and cut in half
1 egg, lightly beaten
2 tablespoons sesame seeds

Preheat the oven to 200°C and line two baking trays with baking paper.

Place the lamb, onion, garlic, harissa, apricots, almonds, coriander leaves and ground spices in a large bowl and combine. Season with a little salt and pepper.

Divide the lamb mixture into 12 equal portions. Place one portion evenly along the longest edge of a pastry sheet, shaping it with a spoon or your fingers. Roll the pastry over to enclose the filling, then brush a little egg along the pastry edge and press to seal. Trim off the excess pastry and repeat with the remaining filling and pastry to make 12 logs.

Brush the logs with egg, scatter with sesame seeds and cut each one into six sausage rolls. Place on the prepared trays and bake for 15–20 minutes or until golden. Serve immediately.

tip

You can store uncooked sausage rolls in an airtight container in the freezer for up to 1 month. Preheat the oven to 200°C and bake them straight from the freezer for 25–30 minutes or until cooked through.

If you've made the mince mixture but can't be bothered to turn it all into sausage rolls, simply form them into golf ball-sized balls to make Middle Eastern meatballs for tapas. Cook in olive oil over medium–high heat for 10–15 minutes or until cooked through.

This is a great way to use up the cauliflower that's rolling around the crisper drawer. Cut it up, bung it in the oven, add a few more ingredients and you've got a warm winter dip that looks fantastic on a grazing table. The subtle Middle Eastern flavours really pair beautifully with the cauliflower.

Warm roasted CAULIFLOWER DIP

Makes about 300 g

1 head of cauliflower, broken into florets
3 tablespoons olive or coconut oil
1½ teaspoons ground coriander
¼ teaspoon ground cumin
pinch of sea salt
3 tablespoons lemon juice
3 tablespoons tahini

TO SERVE
coriander leaves
sesame seeds
extra-virgin olive oil
toasted pita chips

Preheat the oven to 180°C and line a large baking tray with baking paper.

Gently toss together the cauliflower, oil, coriander, cumin and salt until evenly coated. Spread out on the prepared tray and roast, flipping once or twice, for 30–40 minutes or until tender. It will go slightly brown in areas, which is great, but keep an eye on it towards the end of the cooking time because when it turns it can turn quickly!

Remove and set aside to cool slightly before transferring to a food processor. (Do not transfer the cauliflower straight from the oven to the processor as the heat creates pressure, which can crack the processor bowl.) Pulse the cauliflower with the lemon juice and tahini. (Alternatively, you can transfer the cauliflower to a bowl and use a stick blender.) This is not meant to be a smooth dip – I like to leave it nice and chunky!

If you're serving straight away, scoop the cauliflower dip into a serving bowl and scatter with coriander leaves, a sprinkling of sesame seeds and a nice drizzle of olive oil.

If you're making it ahead of time, pop it into an airtight container and store in the fridge for up to 1 day. When you're ready to serve, reheat it gently in a saucepan over low heat and garnish as above.

Serve with toasted pita chips for dipping.

The cobb loaf has come back into fashion in recent years. In fact, I'd be shocked if you went to a barbecue and there wasn't one on the table! This is my mum's recipe and it's always a huge hit. A cobb loaf is a quick and easy starter to bring to a dinner party and looks fantastic on a grazing table. You can choose any sized loaf to hollow out and use as the bowl, just make sure it's dense, such as a sourdough or pana de casa, so that it holds its shape when you add your dip.

Cheese and spinach COBB LOAF

Serves 12

1 sourdough cobb loaf
500 g cream cheese, softened
125 g (½ cup) sour cream
375 g (3 cups) grated cheddar
250 g frozen spinach, thawed and liquid squeezed out
3 spring onions, finely chopped

Preheat the oven to 180°C.

Cut the top off the cobb loaf and, using your hands, dig out the bread. You will be using the torn bread pieces as dippers so tear them out in nice big pieces.

Using a stand or hand-held mixer, beat the cream cheese until smooth. Fold in the sour cream, two-thirds of the grated cheddar, the spinach and spring onion, then spoon the filling into the cobb loaf. Top with the remaining cheddar, place on a large baking tray and bake for 45 minutes.

Arrange the torn bread pieces around the cobb loaf and put it back in the oven for 10 minutes or until the pieces are golden brown, but still soft enough to dip into the gooey cream cheese mixture.

Transfer the cobb loaf to a serving platter and scatter the torn bread around the edge. Once everyone has eaten the dippers, you can make a start on the loaf itself!

‘Throwing a party gets us out from behind our phones and allows us to connect with others – that’s why I will always be so passionate about entertaining.’

People literally go 'oooh!' when I bring this out on a rustic chopping board. Splashing out on a lamb shoulder is one of the best moves I've ever made in the kitchen. Once I realised how easy this is to whip up, I knew it would be my go-to recipe for dinner parties. Sprinkle it with my signature spice rub, chuck it in the oven and you can concentrate on getting everything else ready. I often serve this with flatbreads, coleslaw (see page 153) and tzatziki, and everyone makes their own souvlakis.

Slow-roasted LAMB SHOULDER

Serves 4–6

1 lamb shoulder (about 2 kg), bone in
2 carrots, quartered
4 celery stalks, halved crossways
big bunch of rosemary (stalks and all), plus extra to serve
6 small garlic cloves, peeled
1 heaped tablespoon honey
2 tablespoons olive oil
sea salt

SPICE RUB

1 tablespoon ground cumin
1 tablespoon ground coriander
1 tablespoon freshly ground black pepper
2 teaspoons sweet paprika

PICKLED RED ONION

2 red onions, halved and thinly sliced
1 teaspoon caster sugar
1 teaspoon salt
370 ml light-tasting vinegar (rice, white wine and apple cider vinegar all work well)
a handful of dill sprigs
2 teaspoons black peppercorns

Preheat the oven to 160°C. (If you have an older oven and you know it doesn't have much oomph, then go to 170°C.)

To make the spice rub, mix all the ingredients in a small bowl.

Place the lamb in a colander to drain. If there is any moisture on the top pat it dry with paper towel. Make a bed for the lamb in a roasting tin by covering it with a layer of carrot and celery, then sprinkle over some rosemary. Sit the tin on a tea towel to prevent it from slipping around while you're working on the lamb.

Use a small sharp knife to make six evenly spaced 1–2 cm incisions in the lamb. Push a garlic clove and some sprigs of fresh rosemary into each incision. Drizzle the honey and olive oil over the top, then use your hands to smear it all over the lamb (it's a bit of a cross between dabbing and smearing as the honey kind of comes away from the lamb). Give your hands a wash, then sprinkle the spice rub over the top.

Pour 2 tablespoons of water into the bottom of the tin and triple foil that sucker! By that I mean place one layer of foil over the tin and seal tightly around the edges, then repeat two more times. Whack it in the oven for 4 hours.

Meanwhile, make the pickled red onion. Fill your kettle and put it on to boil, then place the onion in a colander in the sink. Pour the boiling water over the onion to soften it. Combine the sugar, salt and vinegar in a small saucepan and stir over very low heat for a few minutes until the sugar and salt have dissolved. Set aside to cool.

Tear a couple of dill sprigs and add them to the cooled liquid. Transfer the onion to a jar and pour the liquid over the top. Top with the peppercorns and a little more dill, put the lid on and leave to pickle for at least 30 minutes or up to 2 hours.

After 4 hours, take the lamb out of the oven, peel away one edge of the foil and look to see if the meat has shrunk away from the bone. Then check that the meat is nice and tender by pulling at it with a fork – it should fall apart without any effort.

Replace the foil and let the lamb rest for 20 minutes. Just before you're ready to serve, turn your oven up to 220°C, take off the foil and sprinkle some salt over the lamb. Put it back in the oven for 10–15 minutes to brown it all up. Serve with the pickled red onion. Yum!

tip

I often make a triple batch of my signature spice rub to keep in the pantry. It also makes a great Christmas gift. Note that there is no salt in the spice mix, as you don't want to dry the meat out while roasting.

This roast chook is so easy to prep – simply stuff your chicken, marinate and cook. I love to include this on an entertaining menu, alongside my freekeh salad on page 136 or with roast veggies. Of course, you can also cook this chicken on a Sunday or even during the week to feed your family.

Portuguese ROAST CHICKEN

Serves 4

1 x 1.5 kg chicken
½ lemon, cut into thin wedges
100 g butter, cut into cubes
sea salt and freshly ground black pepper
Best Ever Roast Spuds (see page 138), to serve

STUFFING

100 g (1 cup) store-bought chicken stuffing mix (or coarse breadcrumbs mixed with 1 teaspoon dried mixed herbs)
handful of dried cranberries
pinch of sea salt
50 g butter, cut into cubes

MARINADE

2 tablespoons dried oregano
finely grated zest of 1 lemon
2 tablespoons brown sugar
4 garlic cloves, crushed
1 tablespoon store-bought chilli paste or chilli sambal

Preheat the oven to 180°C.

Pat the skin of the chicken dry with paper towel.

To make the stuffing, combine the stuffing mix, cranberries and salt in a bowl. Gradually add about 3 tablespoons of water – just enough to make the mixture wet and firm. Toss through the butter. Now stuff the chicken cavity alternately with the stuffing and the lemon wedges. Tie the legs together using kitchen string, then place in a roasting tin.

To make the marinade, mix all the ingredients in a bowl.

If you have sensitive skin, use kitchen gloves for the next step as the chilli can burn. Gently pull the chicken skin away from the flesh (take care not to tear it) and ease the butter cubes and some of the marinade evenly under the skin. Spread the remaining marinade over the top and bottom of the chicken and season with salt and pepper.

Cover the chicken with foil and pop into the oven for 1 hour or until the chicken is cooked through and the juices run clear when a knife is inserted into the thickest part of the chicken.

Take the chicken out of the oven and let it rest for at least 30 minutes if you can. This will allow all of the juices to run back into the chicken, leaving the flesh soft and succulent.

Increase the oven temperature to 220°C.

Remove the foil from the chicken and pop it back in the oven for 20 minutes to crisp up the skin and give it some colour. Serve with my best ever roast spuds.

‘You do you!’

TYING A TURBAN HEADSCARF

This is one of my most-requested hacks. It's the perfect way to add a splash of colour to a simple outfit or to keep your hair out of your face while you're doing your makeup, or even if you just want to distract the eye away from your messy top-knot on the school run (hey ... no judgment, we've all been there!). Here, I've used three different scarves that complement each other to create interest and height, but one can look just as effective. It's entirely up to you!

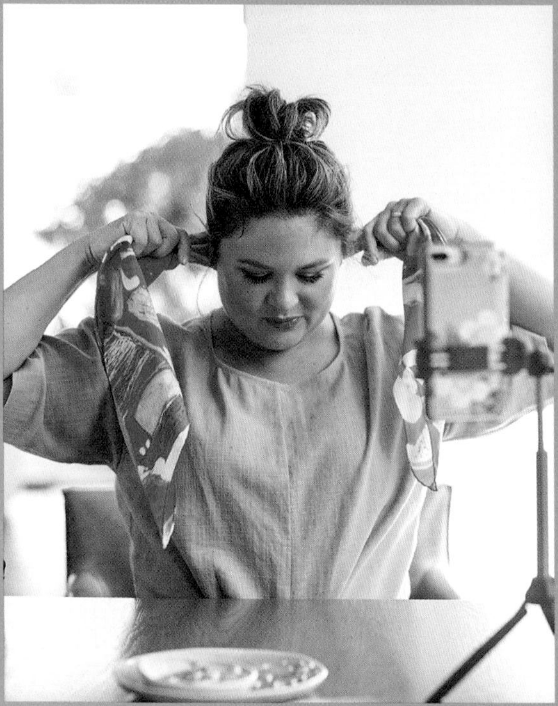

1. Start by folding a square scarf in half to make a triangle with the point at the bottom. Fold the top down twice, then take the bottom point and fold it up. Continue folding until the scarf is about 7–8 cm wide.

2. Now, pick the scarf up and find the midpoint. Place the middle of the scarf at the nape of your neck and bring the two ends up to your crown.

3. Cross the two ends and tie two or three knots to secure.

4. Tuck the loose ends in under the band.

5. Repeat the process with another scarf. I used a long scarf this time, so there was no need to fold it up.

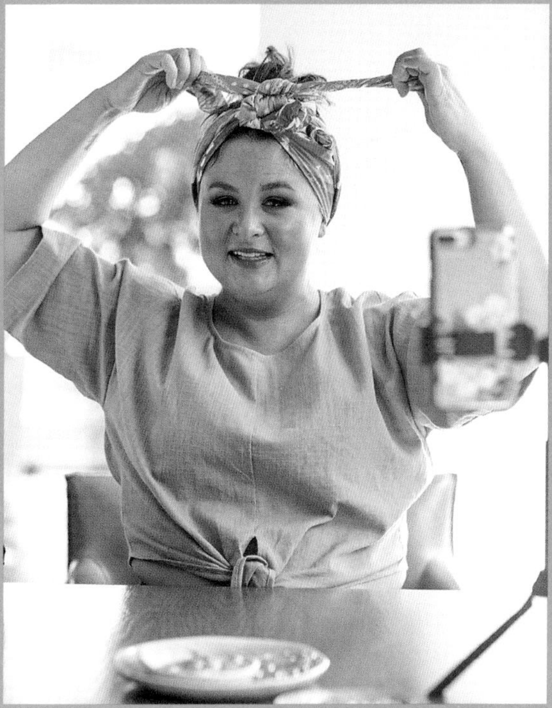

6. Finally, take a third scarf and fold it up so it's quite thin. Thread this scarf through the first two scarves to join them together, then tie a triple knot to secure. Tuck in the ends and you're good to go!

Everyone thinks bao buns are super fancy and mysterious and that you either have to make them from scratch or order them from a restaurant. Not true! They're readily available in the freezer section of most Asian supermarkets. Just chuck them in your steamer for 5–10 minutes and they're ready! This recipe is all about achieving authentic flavours using store-bought ingredients. You can cook the duck legs yourself, but pre-cooked confit duck legs are readily available these days and they make this dish even easier.

DUCK BAO BUNS

with pork crackle and Asian slaw

Makes 6

1 sheet pork skin (from your butcher or supermarket)
sea salt
2 tablespoons char siu sauce
2 store-bought confit duck legs
6 store-bought bao buns

ASIAN SLAW

¼ white cabbage, shredded
¼ purple cabbage, shredded
2 spring onions, thinly sliced
1 carrot, grated
¼ red onion, thinly sliced
good dollop of Japanese mayonnaise (Kewpie)
3 tablespoons chopped mint leaves
3 tablespoons chopped coriander leaves

Preheat the oven to 220°C.

First, get the pork crackle out of the way. Pat the pork skin dry with paper towel, then score it in a criss-cross pattern and place it on a shallow baking tray with a lip. (You don't want the sides of the tray to be too high but you also don't want it to be without a lip, otherwise the oil from the crackle will drip all over your oven.) Pour a motherload of salt on the skin (don't worry – you will dust it off when it's done) and put it in the oven. It should take 20–30 minutes to get it up to full crackle. When it's ready, dust off the salt and chop the crackle into rough, bite-sized pieces.

Reduce the oven temperature to 200°C.

Smear the char siu sauce over the duck legs and place them on a baking tray. Cook in the oven for 15 minutes or until the duck legs are heated through and the skin is looking shiny and plump. Remove and let them cool slightly, then shred the meat off the bone.

Meanwhile, steam the bao buns according to the packet instructions.

Mix all the Asian slaw ingredients in a bowl and you are ready to go!

Open up the bao buns and assemble in this order: Asian slaw, shredded duck and finally a piece of crackle. Yum!

tip

Asian slaw is so easy. If you look super closely you will see it has most of the same ingredients as the Italian coleslaw recipe on page 153. So, if you happen to make the Italian version in the same week, it's good to know you can easily make this one as well!

THE FAST PLATTER

When family or friends drop in unannounced or when the kids bring friends home from school, I like to create what I call my fast platter using food I already have on hand. It's super quick to put together and looks really impressive!

My general rule of thumb is to always include something healthy, something with carbs, something snacky and something sweet. For presentation, I like to use a big board or plate and place everything in little piles. It looks really colourful and it means you only have one thing to wash up. So simple!

When I'm heading out, I love using those old-school Tupperware containers with little sections. So easy, quick and colourful!

HERE ARE SOME OF MY FAVOURITE FAST PLATTER INGREDIENTS:

- Hard-boiled eggs, halved
- Hummus with veggie sticks, such as carrot, celery, cucumber and capsicum
- Cubes of cheese
- Shaved ham or prosciutto
- Sliced kabanosi or kabana
- Popcorn, crackers and mixed nuts
- Fruit, such as grapes or apples and pears, cut into wedges
- Packet-mix or store-bought brownies

PORK SPRING ROLLS

The art of making spring rolls is a cherished tradition in my family, passed down from generation to generation. It occurs every Christmas when the whole family sits down to a massive lunchtime feast of spring rolls and other delights. My mother and older sister were always very much a part of this process with my grandparents and, seeing the love they had for it, I wanted to join in this simple and hugely communal ritual.

I was privileged to step into spring-roll production when I was just six years old. That being said, they only allowed me to separate the pastry wrappers and hand them to my grandparents. After a few years, I slowly moved up the chain of responsibility and was put in charge of peeling the carrots. When I was old enough to hold a knife, I moved up again to chopping the onions. From there, because of the inscrutable eye for perfection of my mother and older sister, I waited years to make my first spring roll. I remained on onion duty until I was eighteen! You could say I did my time and then some.

My grandparents eventually passed, but the family tradition remained, and being of age I was ready to step up. That was until my older brother announced that he would make the spring rolls from now on. It crushed me to say the least. I had spent years and years patiently waiting while my eyes burned with onion tears. The worst part was that my brother had no experience making them! That was when I realised that there is a time to watch and a time to learn and when it comes time to step up, you are the only one who can make it happen. I put my foot down, told my brother if he wanted to help he could pick up a knife and start chopping onions. Rolling spring rolls was now my responsibility! My brother lovingly stepped aside, seeing in my eyes not only my fierce determination but also my love and passion for our family tradition. I owned it, and from that day on, I was in charge.

Three generations of love and passion have gone into these little beauties, so trust me when I say they are the most heart-warming and delicious spring rolls you'll ever make for your friends or family.

RECIPE CONTINUED OVER PAGE >

PORK SPRING ROLLS (CONTINUED)

Makes 35–40

¼ teaspoon sesame oil
1 onion, finely chopped
500 g pork mince
75 g (1 cup) finely chopped cabbage
2 large carrots, grated and chopped
200 g (1½ cups) chopped cooked vermicelli noodles
1 tablespoon kecap manis
1 tablespoon vegetable stock powder (or ½ stock cube, crumbled)
sea salt and freshly ground black pepper
35–40 spring roll wrappers (I use 21.5 cm square wrappers)
2 tablespoons plain flour
500 ml (2 cups) vegetable oil

TO SERVE

iceberg lettuce leaves
Vietnamese mint, coriander and mint leaves
Nuoc Mam Cham (see page 161) or sweet chilli sauce

tip

For vegan spring rolls, replace the pork with 150 g soaked dried shiitake mushrooms, finely chopped, and 200 g firm tofu, finely crumbled. Serve with sweet chilli sauce for dipping.

Heat the sesame oil in a wok or large frying pan over medium heat, add the onion and cook for a few minutes until softened. Add the pork and cook for 5 minutes until browned, breaking up any lumps with a wooden spoon. Throw in the cabbage and carrot and cook, stirring frequently, for about 3 minutes until everything has softened.

Toss through the noodles, then stir in the kecap manis and stock powder and season with salt and pepper. Cook for another 3 minutes or so, then tip the mixture into a colander to drain and cool. That's your filling done.

Get your wrappers out, and mix the flour with about 1 teaspoon of water in a small bowl to make a paste.

Place a wrapper on a flat surface and fold over one end by about 5 cm to create a little reinforced base. Place 2 tablespoons of filling along the folded base, then roll up from the bottom, folding in the sides as you go to form a spring roll. Using your finger, dab a little of the flour paste on the top corners, then roll and press to seal. Place on a tray, then keep going with the remaining wrappers and filling.

Pour the vegetable oil into a large deep saucepan and heat to 180°C. To check whether the oil is ready, pop the end of a wooden spoon into the centre of the oil and if bubbles rise up, you're good to go.

Working in batches of about eight or nine (so you don't overcrowd the pan), add the spring rolls to the oil and cook for 8–10 minutes or until the pastry is golden brown and crunchy. Remove from the oil with a slotted spoon or tongs and set aside to drain on paper towel.

Wrap the hot spring rolls in lettuce leaves with some fresh herbs and serve with nuoc mam cham, sweet chilli or your favourite dipping sauce.

Confidence
and courage
will always be
contagious!

Last year I was lucky enough to share the stage with South African Food Network chef Siba Mtongana and she showed me how to make an amazing pulled pork. This has such a spicy flavour it instantly makes you feel warm and content. Siba smokes her pulled pork to give it an extra dimension, but here I've cooked it in the oven as most people don't have a smoker! The pork is just as delicious.

PULLED PORK
with smoky barbecue sauce

Serves 6–8

80 ml (⅓ cup) olive oil
1 tablespoon sea salt
6 large garlic cloves, finely chopped
2–2.5 kg boneless pork shoulder
coriander leaves, to serve (optional)

SPICE RUB

2 tablespoons smoked paprika
1 tablespoon garlic flakes
1 tablespoon dried chilli flakes
1 teaspoon mustard powder
2 tablespoons brown sugar
2 teaspoons smoked sea salt
1 teaspoon freshly ground black pepper

SMOKY BARBECUE SAUCE

250 ml (1 cup) store-bought smoky barbecue marinade
250 ml (1 cup) warm water
1 teaspoon dijon mustard
1 teaspoon white wine vinegar

Preheat the oven to 140°C.

Rub the oil, salt and garlic all over the pork.

To make the spice rub, combine all the ingredients in a small bowl.

Heat a large flameproof casserole dish over medium–high heat. Place the pork in the dish and sear it on all sides for 5–10 minutes, until well browned.

Remove the dish from the heat and, using a spatula, smear the spice rub all over the pork.

To make the barbecue sauce, mix all the ingredients in a small bowl.

Pour half the sauce over the meat, then cover and place in the oven for 4 hours, adding the remaining sauce halfway through cooking.

When the meat is cooked through and pulls away easily, take it out of the oven and let it cool for 15 minutes. You only want the meat to cool slightly – it pulls better while it's still warm.

Use two forks to pull the pork apart, then return it to the dish and mix with the pan juices and sprinkle over some coriander leaves, if you like.

I like to serve the pulled pork with my orange, spinach and cranberry salad on page 147, but it is also perfect served in sliders, burgers and wraps. The options are endless!

BRONZER: THE MAGIC NUMBER 3

Remember back in the day when we used to slap on a tonne of matte-mousse foundation, heavy eyeliner and sparkly lip gloss before heading out on the town? Well, thank God those days are over, and we now have fantastic makeup tutorials at our disposal to make sure we never again show up in photos with ghostly light, featureless faces! I often get feedback that people don't know what to do with bronzer. While there are loads of different ways to use it, here's my favourite method to accent the cheekbones and give your face a sun-kissed glow.

1. Apply your usual foundation.

2. Take a large makeup brush, swirl it over your bronzer and tap off any excess. Go light with your first round, you can always add more.

3. Here's where the magic number 3 comes in! Slightly flatten the brush with your fingers. Begin at the forehead and sweep around your face under your cheekbone, then sweep out along the cheekbone again and down under your chin (making a 3 shape).

4. Repeat on the other side. If you feel you need a bit more, here's where you can go over it again until you're happy with the colour.

5. Once your bronzer is complete, apply a hint of your favourite blush on the roses of your cheeks.

The scent of this aromatic marinade always takes me straight back to Thailand. I can instantly recall the people, colours, noises, smells and, of course, the incredible food. This is one of my favourite Thai dishes, and I love the way the pork melts in your mouth. These skewers are a real crowd pleaser, especially in summer when the barbecue is always firing.

MOO PING PORK SKEWERS

Serves 4

500 g pork shoulder, cut into thin strips (see tip)
Thai basil leaves, to serve

MARINADE

4 garlic cloves, peeled
1 lemongrass stalk, white part only, finely chopped
pinch of sea salt
1 tablespoon finely chopped coriander stalks
½ teaspoon ground white pepper
80 ml (⅓ cup) coconut milk
1 tablespoon soy sauce
2 tablespoons fish sauce
2 teaspoons oyster sauce
2 tablespoons grated palm sugar
2 teaspoons vegetable oil

tip

Make life easy and pop the pork in the freezer for 30 minutes before cutting. The knife will glide through, allowing you to cut nice even strips of meat.

For a more authentic flavour, you can try cooking these skewers over coals.

To make the marinade, place the garlic, lemongrass and salt in a mortar and pound with the pestle to create a paste. Combine with the remaining ingredients in a bowl.

Put the pork in a glass or ceramic dish, pour over the marinade and turn to coat. Cover and refrigerate for at least couple of hours (overnight is better!).

About 30 minutes before you are ready to start cooking, soak 16 small wooden skewers in water to stop them burning during cooking.

Thread the pork onto the soaked skewers.

Heat a chargrill pan over medium–high heat or a barbecue grill plate to medium–hot. Place the skewers in the pan or on the barbecue and sear for 1 minute on each side, then reduce the heat to low and cook, turning often, for about 10 minutes or until cooked through. You want the fat in the pork to melt and become buttery.

Scatter over some Thai basil leaves and serve with my spicy som tum (see page 148) and sticky rice (see page 57) as part of a Thai banquet.

Don't you just love having a house full of people? The noise, the clink of wine glasses, a movie blaring in the background and kids running everywhere. At some point, you realise everyone is starving and you forgot to organise dinner. Don't stress! Instead of spending a fortune on takeaway, why not get everyone to pitch in and make this massive homemade pizza together? It's a quick, delicious recipe that feeds a tribe and can be whipped up with one hand still on your wine glass (especially if you're clever enough to have it pre-prepared in the freezer).

THE PARTY PIZZA

Serves 8

1 long loaf Turkish bread
3 tablespoons good-quality pizza sauce
2 bacon rashers, chopped
1 red capsicum, deseeded and diced
2 tomatoes, seeds scooped out and diced
1 corn cob, husk and silks removed, kernels cut off
large handful of baby spinach, roughly chopped
½ small red onion, finely diced
150 g (1 cup) grated mozzarella or pizza cheese
1 egg
sea salt and freshly ground black pepper

Preheat the oven to 180°C. Line a large baking tray with baking paper.

Place the Turkish bread on a clean work surface and trim any doughy bumps off the top of the Turkish bread – you want the bread to be an even thickness. If necessary, slice the Turkish bread in half so it fits in your oven. Spread the pizza sauce over the bread.

Mix the bacon, capsicum, tomato, corn, spinach, onion and cheese in a large bowl. Crack in the egg and stir it through to coat everything, then season well with salt and pepper. Tip the mixture onto the Turkish bread and spread out evenly.

Transfer the Turkish bread to the prepared tray and bake for 20 minutes or until the crust is crisp, the egg is cooked and the cheese is melted and bubbling. Serve immediately.

tip

For a sneaky timesaving trick, put all the ingredients (except the bread, pizza sauce and egg) into a zip-lock bag in the freezer. Pull it out and leave to defrost, add the egg and you're good to go!

For a vegan version, simply omit the bacon and egg, and use vegan cheese instead of mozzarella.

HOW TO NAIL THE PERFECT BROW

You have no idea how many requests I get about brows. I usually visit a brow bar to get mine done, but sometimes there's just no time and I need to do them myself. So, here are my tips on how to smash out the perfect brow every time.

Remember, your eyebrows are YOUR eyebrows. Choose the right shape for you.

If you don't have time to get a professional tint done, there are loads of products out there to help you fill your brows like a pro.

Your brow brush is you friend. When brushing your brows, brush in an upward direction, then run the brush along the top of your brow to create a line.

Use a brow pencil that matches your brow colour.

If you don't have a brow pencil, use a small makeup brush and a little eyeshadow.

Don't use too much product on the thicker end of your brow, just a light touch and blend with your brow brush.

After filling, use some concealer on a small flat brush to run under your brow to tidy up any fallout.

If you have unruly brows (firstly ... lucky you!), you can now get brow gels, pomades and other products to help you tame them.

If you are on the other end of the spectrum and you don't have much of a brow, microblading can be a great option to give your brows some definition and colour.

The only thing worse than soggy crackling is burnt crackling. It's gotta be perfect or you might as well throw the whole lot in the bin and go to bed. I'm going to let you in on a little secret: did you know that you can buy pork skin separately from most butchers? It's brilliant. The trick is to buy more than you need so you can make a double batch. Alternatively, ask your butcher to remove the skin from your pork belly, as I have done here. I tend to cook my crackling before I even put the pork in the oven. That way it's ready whenever you are, and you only need to warm it up before serving.

I love to serve this porchetta with my best ever roast spuds (see page 138) and favourite roast veggies or my apple and fennel slaw (see page 158).

PORCHETTA *with* PERFECT PORK CRACKLE

Serves 8

2–2.5 kg boneless pork belly (see tip)

PORK CRACKLE

pork skin, removed from pork belly
sea salt
olive oil, for rubbing

PORK RUB

3 tablespoons finely chopped sage leaves
3 tablespoons finely chopped rosemary leaves
finely grated zest of 1 large orange (reserve the orange for the veggie trivet)
finely grated zest of 1 lemon (reserve the lemon for the veggie trivet)
1 tablespoon dijon mustard
1 tablespoon seeded mustard
3 tablespoons olive oil
3 garlic cloves, crushed
1 tablespoon dried oregano

VEGGIE TRIVET

any veggies you have in the crisper drawer (carrot, celery, onion and sweet potato all work well)
reserved orange and lemon from the rub

tip

Ask your butcher to take off the pork skin for you. You want it to come off without removing the fat from the meat. Or you can do it yourself if you're confident.

Let's get the pork crackle out of the way. Pat dry the pork skin with paper towel and gently score the skin. Leave it on your work surface for a couple of hours to dry out.

Crank your oven to 220°C.

Transfer the pork skin to a roasting tin, cover the skin with plenty of salt and rub in a little olive oil, making sure to really get in those scored lines. Roast in the oven for 45 minutes or until the skin is completely dry and crisp. Set aside to cool while you get on with the porchetta.

Reduce the oven temperature to 150°C.

To make the pork rub, mix all the ingredients in a bowl. Remove about one-quarter of the rub and set it aside for later.

Turn the pork belly fat-side down and very lightly slash the meat with a sharp knife, then massage the rub into the cuts.

Cut some lengths of kitchen string and get ready to ROLL! Now roll up the pork belly and secure with string at even intervals. Massage the reserved rub over the outside of the pork.

To make the veggie trivet, arrange the veggies, orange and lemon in the bottom of a large roasting tin. Sit the pork belly on top, then pop it in the oven. The roasting time will vary depending on the weight of the pork, but the basic rule of thumb is 30 minutes per 500 g of pork belly, so you're looking at 2½–3 hours. Skewer the thickest part of the meat – if the juices run clear the pork is cooked.

Take the pork out and put it on a board. Cover loosely with foil and let it rest for at least 45 minutes to allow all of the juices to go back into the meat. I can't stress the importance of this step enough. All the marinade and prepping in the world won't give you the succulent result you're after if you don't rest the meat properly. Towards the end of this resting time, pop the pork crackle back in the oven to warm up.

Cut the porchetta into thick slices and serve with shards of the pork crackle, my roast spuds, your favourite roast veggies, or apple and fennel slaw.

EMMYLOU'S LIFE HACKS

HOW TO CREATE THE PERFECT RED LIP

Mastering a bold red lip can be a challenge. Get it wrong and you can end up with smudged lines and lipstick-stained teeth. Instead, follow these simple steps for a smokin' red lip that looks killer and ain't going anywhere.

1. Apply a really moisturising lip balm to your lips (coconut oil works well). Leave it on for 5 minutes.

2. Use a clean, soft toothbrush to gently buff your lips in a circular motion to remove any dry, dead skin. Gently wipe with a tissue to remove any excess lip balm.

3. Using small, feathery strokes, start to line your lips with your favourite lip liner. Line your top lip using upward strokes and your bottom lip using downward strokes (this follows your natural collagen lines).

4. Use your favourite lipstick to fill in your lips with colour.

5. To make sure you don't end up with lipstick on your teeth, place a finger in your mouth, suck your finger and pull it out. It's an old-school trick, but it works every time.

6.

KNOCK 'EM DEAD!

SALADS *and* VEGETABLES

Simple, fresh and punchy!

If you want a show-stopping dish that can be eaten as a side or on its own, you can't go past my freekeh salad. You can double, triple or even quadruple the quantity to feed a tribe and it won't compromise the flavours. This is, hands down, one of my most popular salads and I love serving it alongside my slow-roasted lamb shoulder (see page 92). Bring it to your next barbecue and I guarantee you'll be asked to share the recipe (and no, you can't take credit for it!).

FREEKEH SALAD
with cranberry dressing

Serves 4–6 as a side

40 g butter
2 small shallots, finely chopped
200 g (1 cup) cracked freekeh, rinsed and drained a couple of times
500 ml (2 cups) vegetable stock
175 g (1 cup) coarse bulgur
handful of mint leaves, finely chopped
handful of flat-leaf parsley leaves, finely chopped
handful of roasted almonds, roughly chopped
2 preserved lemon skins, finely chopped (or finely grated zest of 1 lemon)
250 g feta, crumbled

CRANBERRY DRESSING
80 g dried cranberries
2 teaspoons white wine vinegar
2 tablespoons olive oil

To make the cranberry dressing, place the cranberries in a small saucepan with 250 ml (1 cup) of water and bring to the boil over high heat. Reduce the heat to low and simmer for about 5 minutes until the liquid has reduced slightly. Leave to cool, then transfer to a bowl and stir through the vinegar and oil.

Melt the butter in a large saucepan over medium heat. Add the shallot and freekeh and cook, stirring, for 2–3 minutes or until the freekeh is slightly toasted and the shallot is translucent.

Pour in the veggie stock and bring to the boil. Reduce the heat to low, put the lid on and leave for 15 minutes, stirring only once. (When you first cook this, you will want to keep checking it as it behaves slightly differently to rice, but you will get used to it and before long you and freekeh will be firm friends!) Once the freekeh is tender and all the stock has been absorbed, remove it from the heat, leave the lid on and set aside for another 15 minutes.

Meanwhile, combine the bulgur and 500 ml (2 cups) of water in a saucepan. Bring to the boil over medium heat and cook for about 12 minutes, until tender and the liquid has been absorbed. Remove from the heat and fluff the grains up with a fork.

Pop the freekeh in a large bowl and set aside to cool. Add the cooked bulgur, chopped herbs, almonds and lemon and toss well to combine. Transfer to a serving bowl, pour over the cranberry dressing and gently toss through. Finish with the crumbled feta, toss again and serve.

If you are looking for the most delicious and decadent potatoes to serve with your weekly roast, you have come to the right place. The secret to making spuds that are golden and crisp on the outside yet fluffy on the inside is to soak them in cold water for a few hours, then parboil them before roasting. You will never need another roast potato recipe again!

Best ever ROAST SPUDS

Serves 4 as a side

8 large, dirty potatoes
olive oil, for drizzling
sea salt
a few rosemary sprigs, leaves picked

Peel your spuds and give them a rinse, then cut them in half. If you have time, soak them in cold water for 2 hours to remove some of the excess starch. Don't worry if not; I've been in a rush and given them a mini soak for 5 minutes and they still come out just fine.

Put the potatoes in a large saucepan of fresh cold water and bring to the boil, then simmer until they are just cooked through. The cooking time will vary, depending on size, but if you have a million things going on, just set your timer for 15 minutes or so, then keep checking every 5 minutes from there. You don't want to let them bubble away and turn into mash!

As soon as you can get a fork most of the way through a test spud, tip them into a colander and give them a little jostle, then arrange them on a wire rack. You are going to leave these guys until they are totally cold and dry. It actually doesn't take that long – the steam seems to dry them and being on the rack lets them cool pretty quickly.

When you are about 40 minutes away from serving, preheat the oven to 220°C.

Grab your favourite roasting tin and pour in a good slug of olive oil (you actually want to coat your potatoes, so it's probably a little more than you're used to using). Gently toss the cold potatoes in the oil. Season well with salt, scatter over the rosemary leaves and roast for about 30 minutes, turning or tossing them halfway through. Be patient; if they are still a bit pale, give them another 10–15 minutes until they are golden and crispy on the outside, fluffy on the inside and completely addictive. Enjoy! (I know you will.)

Oh parsnip. You poor, neglected little veggie. It always surprises me when people say they don't eat parsnips ... because they're the same people who go nuts for it when I put these parsnip chips on my winter grazing table! Trust me when I say you can never make enough of them. They go like hotcakes and they're so easy to make. Toss with oil, roll in the crumb and roast until crisp. Done.

Crumbed PARSNIP CHIPS

Serves 4 as a side

8 parsnips, peeled and cut into even wedges or thick batons
80 ml (⅓ cup) olive or coconut oil
120 g (2 cups) panko breadcrumbs
sea salt

Preheat the oven to 180°C and line a large baking tray with baking paper.

Mix the parsnip and oil in a large bowl until the parsnip is well coated.

Tip the breadcrumbs into a shallow bowl, season with salt and add the parsnip. Turn to coat evenly.

Arrange the parsnip on the prepared tray in a single layer and bake for 20–30 minutes or until golden and tender. Serve hot.

tip

To save on prep time, crumb the parsnips a few hours ahead and set aside in the fridge until you're ready to cook them.

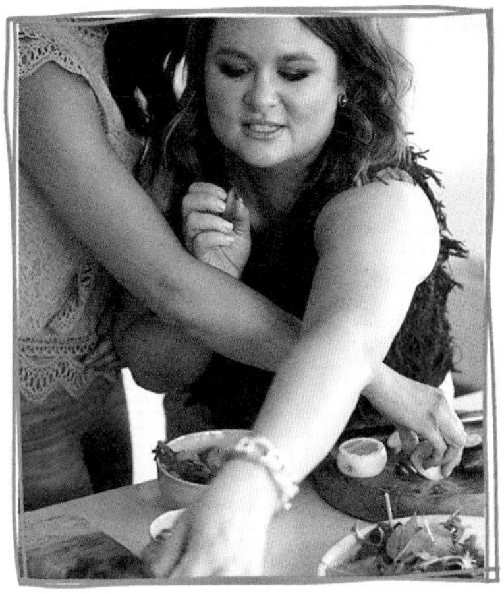

The trick to getting broccolini super green and crisp is to blanch it first. Blanching locks in the colour and the nutrients and gives it a crunch that is normally reserved for cafes and restaurants!

ZESTY BROCCOLINI *with slivered almonds*

Serves 4 as a side

2 bunches of broccolini, halved lengthways or left whole
ice cubes
50 g butter
40 g (⅓ cup) slivered almonds
1½ teaspoons finely grated lemon zest
lemon wedges, to serve
sea salt and freshly ground black pepper

Bring a large saucepan of water to the boil. Throw in the broccolini and pop on the lid.

Quickly prepare an ice bath by filling a large bowl with cold water and adding a big handful of ice cubes. Place it in the sink. By the time you've done this (2–3 minutes max) your broccolini should be done. Drain it in a colander, then tip it straight into the ice bath. Let it cool for 5 minutes, then drain.

Melt the butter in a large frying pan over medium–high heat. When it starts to froth a little, toss in the broccolini, almonds and lemon zest. Give it all a couple of fancy tosses in the pan (you know, the ones where all the vegetables are sure to spill all over your stovetop) and you're done!

Jostle it onto your serving dish, making sure some of those golden almonds are sprinkled deliciously over the top. Finish off with a squeeze of lemon and some salt and pepper and serve immediately.

This winter salad is light, fresh and full of citrus punch. I love to make the most of oranges when they're in season, and this dish is a great way to put them on show. The bright orange looks incredible against the green baby spinach and you've got that lovely crunch from the almonds.

ORANGE, SPINACH *and* CRANBERRY SALAD

Serves 4 as a side

280 g baby spinach leaves
4–6 navel oranges, segmented
1 large red apple, cored and julienned or shredded
60 g (½ cup) dried cranberries
40 g (⅓ cup) slivered almonds (walnuts are good too)

DRESSING

3 tablespoons orange juice
finely grated zest of 1 orange
¼ teaspoon sea salt
3 tablespoons extra-virgin olive oil
2 tablespoons caster sugar
1 tablespoon apple cider vinegar or white wine vinegar
2 teaspoons lemon juice

To make the dressing, place all the ingredients in a jar, pop on the lid and give it a good shake.

Place all the salad ingredients in a bowl, add the dressing and gently toss to coat.

Serve as part of a grazing table with the pulled pork (see page 114). These two are dynamite together.

I've spent a lot of time in Thailand over the years. It's a place that brings me a sense of calm and restores my balance. Whether training at a Muay Thai camp or meditating at a yoga retreat, I've always tried to experience as much of the local cuisine as possible. I love recreating my favourite Thai dishes at home and you'll be surprised how easy it is to source traditional Thai ingredients, such as green papaya, which is the hero in this salad.

Spicy SOM TUM

Serves 4 as a side

2 garlic cloves, crushed
1–2 small Thai green or red chillies (to taste), finely chopped
2 tablespoons roasted peanuts
2 tablespoons dried shrimp (optional)
180 g (2 cups) grated green papaya
3–4 snake beans (see tip)
1 carrot, grated (optional)
2 tablespoons fish sauce (see tip)
8 cherry tomatoes, halved
juice of 1½ limes
½ teaspoon grated palm sugar (or raw sugar if you can't find it)
¼ teaspoon sea salt

Grab a mortar and pestle. (If you don't have one, a metal bowl and the end of a rolling pin will do the job!) Pound the garlic and chilli, then add the nuts and shrimp (if using) and pound a few more times.

For the next part you need both hands and a little bit of Thai grit! Add the remaining ingredients to the mortar and quickly bruise the salad. Grab a spoon, then continue to pound with the pestle and mix with the spoon until the salad is completely combined and coated in the chilli paste and Thai flavours.

Transfer the salad to a large serving bowl, give everything a final toss and serve immediately.

tip

Snake beans are very long green beans that are popular in South East Asia. You can buy them at Asian supermarkets.

You can use soy sauce instead of fish sauce and omit the shrimp to make a vegan version of this recipe.

This is another recipe from my sister Suc-Lyn. It is a twist on the classic backyard barbecue side dish, and is zesty, flavourful and sure to be a favourite all summer long. If you have a mandoline use it to make quick work of slicing your veggies.

My sister's ITALIAN COLESLAW

Serves 4 as a side

¼ white cabbage, shredded
½ baby fennel bulb, trimmed and thinly sliced
¼ red onion, thinly sliced
2 radishes, thinly sliced
3 tablespoons torn mint leaves
3 tablespoons torn flat-leaf parsley leaves
handful of fresh peas
grated parmesan, to serve

DRESSING

3 tablespoons olive oil
2 tablespoons lemon juice
3 tablespoons finely grated parmesan
sea salt and freshly ground black pepper

First make the dressing. Grab a salad bowl, pour in the olive oil and lemon juice, add the parmesan and give it all a good mix. Season to taste with salt and pepper.

Place the veggies and herbs in the bowl. Just before you're ready to serve, give it all a toss to coat the veggies in the dressing.

Scatter the peas over the top and finish with a sprinkling of parmesan.

I met Colin and his wife, Jane, at the Grape Escape Festival in The Grampians in Victoria. I watched him cook this whole pumpkin for the crowd and was completely awestruck. It's everything I love in a recipe: tasty, beautiful, simple and it uses the entire vegetable. This is a real showstopper. Colin has been kind enough to let me share this recipe with you. Legend.

Colin Fassnidge's WHOLE ROAST PUMPKIN

Serves 8–10 as a side

1 medium kent pumpkin
3 tablespoons olive oil
sea salt
4 garlic cloves, peeled and bruised
1 large red chilli, thickly sliced
1 lemon, cut into wedges
4 rosemary sprigs, roughly torn, plus extra sprigs to decorate (optional)

Preheat the oven to 180°C. Line a large baking tray with baking paper.

Cut the top off the pumpkin. Using a large spoon, scoop out the centre and the seeds. Drizzle the olive oil over the pumpkin inside and out (including the top), then grind some sea salt into your hand and rub the oil and salt all over.

Grab the garlic cloves and rub them on the inside of the pumpkin, then drop them into the centre along with the chilli, lemon wedges and rosemary.

Place on the prepared tray and bake for 45 minutes. Place the oiled pumpkin lid upside-down on the tray next to the pumpkin and bake for another 35 minutes.

Transfer the pumpkin to a serving platter and arrange some extra sprigs of rosemary around the outside to decorate, if you like. Place in the centre of your table and accept all the glorious compliments coming your way!

'Love h

hard, p

d, work
y hard!'

This is such a simple, crisp salad and it goes beautifully with my pulled pork (see page 114). I find pork to be quite heavy, so even though I love it with roast veggies, I appreciate it even more when it's served with a nice fresh apple slaw.

APPLE *and* FENNEL SLAW

Serves 6 as a side

4 large green apples, cored and thinly sliced
2 large red apples, cored and thinly sliced
1 small red onion, thinly sliced
1 fennel bulb, trimmed and thinly sliced (reserve some fronds to serve)
juice of ½ lemon

DRESSING

2 tablespoons apple cider vinegar
3 tablespoons olive oil
1 tablespoon dijon mustard
2 teaspoons sugar

To make the dressing, whisk all the ingredients in a small bowl, making sure the sugar has completely dissolved.

Prepare the slaw ingredients, squeezing a little lemon juice over them as you go to stop them browning.

Transfer the slaw ingredients to a serving bowl or platter. Just before you are ready to serve, add the dressing, toss to combine and top with some fennel fronds. Simple!

tip

If you have one, use a mandoline to get really lovely uniform slices but please be careful with your fingers and use the safety guard.

This is a super-easy dish to make! All you need to do is mix your ingredients and dress with homemade nuoc mam cham. Start off light with the dressing as it can be quite strong, but as you get a taste for Vietnamese flavours you will discover where your limit is. This salad is fantastic to take to a barbecue as it works well with grilled meats. My oldest brother Khanh loves to get a bowl of this and add cut-up freshly cooked spring rolls. It's such a traditional Vietnamese thing to do and it tastes fab!

VIETNAMESE SALAD *with nuoc mam cham*

Serves 6–8 as a side

200 g thin dried rice noodles
225 g (3 cups) shredded red and white cabbage
180 g (2 cups) shredded or julienned carrot
120 g (3 cups) mixed lettuce leaves
180 g (2 cups) bean sprouts
1 continental cucumber, seeds removed, sliced
handful of mixed herbs (basil, Vietnamese mint, mint and garlic chives all work well)
sliced long red chilli, to serve

NUOC MAM CHAM

220 g (1 cup) caster sugar, dissolved in 250 ml (1 cup) water
2–3 long red chillies, roughly chopped
3 garlic cloves, roughly chopped
sea salt
250 ml (1 cup) fish sauce
125 ml (½ cup) lemon juice
80 ml (⅓ cup) white vinegar

tip

This nuoc mam cham will keep for, like, EVER! Just store it in a jar in the fridge. In addition to being a traditional Vietnamese salad dressing, it can be used as a dipping sauce for spring rolls and rice paper rolls. It's also lovely spooned over grilled fish with steamed rice!

First, make your nuoc mam cham. Get yourself a large clean glass jar that can hold around 1 litre of liquid and pour in the dissolved sugar.

Grab your chilli and garlic and pop them into a mortar. Pound them up with a pestle until nice and fine. Add a pinch of salt at this point to help create a paste. Transfer the paste to the jar, add the fish sauce, lemon juice and vinegar, give it a good shake and you are done!

Cook the rice noodles according to the packet instructions. Drain and allow to cool, then roughly chop.

Combine the cabbage, carrot, lettuce, bean sprouts, cucumber, herbs and chopped noodles in a large bowl. Add a little nuoc mam cham and toss to coat. Taste and add more until it tastes right to you, then serve straight away with sliced chilli and nuoc mam cham on the side.

Every decent barbecue will have a potato salad (or three) on the table. Show up to a party in the same outfit? Disaster. Show up to a party and you're both carrying a potato salad? High fives all round. This particular potato salad is guaranteed to get the party started. It's my brother Kim-Lee's recipe and I can still remember the first day he made it. Roasting the potatoes with their skins on was a revelation and I think we ate this every night for about two weeks! If you've never made your own mayo, I encourage you to give this a try. It's so good that when Kim-Lee first taught me how to make it I went on a bit of a mayo rampage and used it in everything. If you knew me back in the day, I definitely would have made this potato salad for you.

ROASTED POTATO *and* CHORIZO SALAD

Serves 8

1.2 kg baby potatoes, quartered
2 tablespoons olive oil
sea salt and freshly ground black pepper
2 raw chorizo sausages, roughly chopped
1 red onion, halved and thinly sliced
1 spring onion, sliced on the diagonal
2 large handfuls of rocket leaves

STICK-BLENDER MAYO

1 egg, at room temperature
1 tablespoon white wine vinegar (or lemon or lime juice)
1 teaspoon dijon or seeded mustard
350 ml vegetable oil
pinch of sea salt

tip

Don't make this mayo with olive oil as the flavour is too overpowering.

For a richer mayo, add 1–2 egg yolks (save the whites for another use).

For a quick aioli, add a teaspoon or so of crushed garlic to the mayo.

If the mayo splits during blending start again, but use the split product instead of the vegetable oil. It won't be quite the same but it will still taste great and is better than wasting the ingredients.

Preheat the oven to 180°C and line a large baking tray with baking paper.

Place the potato and olive oil in a large bowl, season with salt and pepper and toss to coat well. Spread out on the prepared tray and roast for 30 minutes. Add the chorizo and cook for a further 10 minutes, or until the potato is cooked through and golden brown and the chorizo is nice and crisp.

While your potatoes and chorizo are roasting, make the mayo. Put all the ingredients in a narrow beaker or jug. Start with the stick blender at the bottom and blend for 3–5 seconds or until everything comes together, then slowly pull the blender to the top. Now use an up and down motion to finish the mayonnaise. This process should only take 10–15 seconds. DONE!

Remove the potato and chorizo from the oven and leave to cool completely. (If you don't wait for them to cool before adding the mayo, it'll melt and make an oily mess!) Once cool, transfer to a large mixing bowl along with the red onion. Add the mayo a little at a time and gently toss to combine until you reach your desired potato to mayo ratio. Taste and add more seasoning if you think it needs it.

Transfer the salad to a serving bowl, scatter over the spring onion and rocket and you're good to go. Any leftover mayo will keep in an airtight container in the fridge for up to 1 week.

PORTRAIT

DESSERTS

Showstopper sweets that will win you friends!

I started making these jaffle pies when I was 14 and living out of home. They are sweet, simple and ridiculously naughty – perfect for a teenage cook! I still love this dessert just as much as an adult and enjoy experimenting with different flavours. Try other canned fruits, such as peaches, or mix up the flavour of the jam and ground spices – ginger and nutmeg work really well too.

JAFFLE APPLE PIES
with salted caramel sauce

Serves 4

2 sheets frozen puff pastry
butter, for spreading
385 g can pie fruit apples
raspberry jam, for spreading
ground cinnamon, for dusting
ice cream, to serve
icing sugar, to serve

SALTED CARAMEL SAUCE
220 g (1 cup) sugar
70 g butter
185 ml (¾ cup) pouring cream
1 teaspoon sea salt
1 teaspoon ground cinnamon

To make the salted caramel sauce, melt the sugar in a saucepan over medium heat. If you haven't done this before, simply stir with a wooden spoon and don't panic if the sugar gets a little clumpy. Just keep going until the sugar melts and turns a dark amber. The colour is super important when you're first starting out, as sugar can burn pretty easily, so keep an eye on it and watch for that gorgeous amber colour.

As soon as it gets to that point, add the butter and stir for 2–3 minutes or until melted. You can use a whisk if you find the butter is separating from the sugar.

While continuing to stir, add the cream in a thin, steady stream. Cook for a further minute and watch the mixture bubble up in the pan. Remove from the heat and stir through the salt and cinnamon. Don't skip this step – the salt is what makes it so amazing! Allow the sauce to cool while you make the pies.

Preheat your jaffle maker.

Get the puff pastry out of the freezer when you're ready to use it (you don't want it to go all floppy as it just doesn't cook as well). Cut each pastry sheet into four squares about the same size as a slice of bread.

Butter one side of each pastry square and place four of them, butter-side down, in the jaffle maker (if your jaffle maker only cooks two at once you'll need to do this in batches). Spread a couple of spoonfuls of apple over the pastry and add some jam if you want extra sweetness or even just a sprinkle of cinnamon. Place the remaining pastry squares on top, butter-side up. Close your jaffle maker and give it a good 10 minutes or so, until the pastry is golden. That's it!

Serve the pies with your favourite ice cream and a dusting of icing sugar. Pour over the caramel sauce and get back to the couch!

The first time I tasted this dessert, I was studying beauty therapy in Perth and a friend invited me to her house for dinner. I was super broke at the time and here I was in this fancy house where the whole family sat at the table and told witty jokes while they tucked into their steak and veggies. I felt like I was on the set of Family Ties! When my friend's mum brought out brandied oranges for dessert I almost fell off my chair. It was just about the most elegant thing I'd ever seen.

I spent years trying to recreate this dish and once I'd mastered it, there was no turning back. It's best to make it in winter when oranges are in season because they are sweet and juicy, allowing you to showcase this beautiful ingredient without breaking a sweat. It makes the ideal weekend dessert.

BRANDIED ORANGES with whipped cream

Serves 10

410 g caster sugar
1 cinnamon stick
10 oranges
4 tablespoons brandy
2½ tablespoons orange liqueur (such as Cointreau)
whipped cream or coconut yoghurt, to serve

Place the sugar and cinnamon stick in a small saucepan, add 300 ml of water and stir over low heat until the sugar has dissolved. Increase the heat and boil for 2 minutes, then remove from the heat and allow to cool slightly. Remove the cinnamon stick.

While the sugar syrup is cooling, get on with prepping your citrus.

Peel the oranges, making sure you remove all the white pith (that stuff can really mess with the taste!) and thinly slice crossways. You can cut the oranges into segments if you like, but crossways is quicker and easier if this is your first crack. If there are any pips, remove them carefully. Transfer to a serving bowl.

Pour the brandy, orange liqueur and sugar syrup over the prepared oranges and leave to sit for at least 30 minutes, although you can actually leave this overnight.

Serve at room temperature with a generous dollop of whipped cream or coconut yoghurt.

I always forget that this is a vegan dish! It's so delicious that you should probably make enough for everyone. I love that you can sauté the apple on the stove then bung it all in the oven. Serve it with fresh coconut cream and your plant-loving friends will be over the moon.

Vegan apple and berry CRUMBLE

Serves 6

2 tablespoons coconut oil or vegan butter
8 large green apples, peeled, cored and sliced
1 teaspoon ground cinnamon
juice of ½ orange
125 g (1 cup) frozen mixed berries
sea salt

THE CRUMB

150 g (1½ cups) rolled oats
3 tablespoons brown sugar
3 tablespoons coconut oil or vegan butter
handful of slivered almonds
handful of chopped dates
3 tablespoons shredded coconut

WHIPPED COCONUT CREAM

2 x 400 ml cans coconut cream (see tip)
1 tablespoon coconut oil
1 tablespoon maple syrup
1 teaspoon vanilla extract

tip

Choose a brand of coconut cream that is 100% coconut with no added water. For best results, place the cans upside-down in the fridge overnight. This makes it easier to separate the liquid and the cream. Alternatively, use coconut yoghurt instead of cream.

If you don't have an ovenproof frying pan, transfer the filling to a baking dish, sprinkle with the crumb and salt, and bake as directed.

Preheat the oven to 180°C.

To make the crumb, place the oats and brown sugar in a bowl, add the coconut oil or vegan butter and rub it in with your fingertips. Stir in the almonds, dates and shredded coconut. Set aside while you prepare the apple filling.

Melt the coconut oil or vegan butter in a large ovenproof frying pan over medium heat. Throw in the apple, sprinkle over the cinnamon and cook for 8 minutes or until the apple starts to soften. Squeeze in the orange juice and stir. Add the berries and cook for a further 3 minutes. Remove the pan from the heat.

Quickly sprinkle the crumb over the top of the fruit, along with a pinch of salt. Pop the pan in the oven and bake for 20–30 minutes or until the crumble is lovely and golden and the apple is tender. Take out of the oven and leave to cool for 10 minutes.

Meanwhile, to make the whipped coconut cream, open the cans of coconut cream and scoop only the hard cream on top into a bowl (save the remaining liquid to add to smoothies if you like). Add the coconut oil, maple syrup and vanilla, then beat with a hand-held mixer until well combined.

Serve the crumble warm with a good dollop of whipped coconut cream.

ICE CREAM SANDWICHES

Who doesn't love ice cream sandwiches? They're bloody delicious in my book and they make a fabulous speedy dessert that can be put together in seconds. The best part is you can mix and match your favourite biscuits and ice cream! Here's how I do it.

Hold a biscuit in your hand with the base facing upwards – I like to use Choc Ripple biscuits. Using a dessertspoon, generously scoop some ice cream onto the biscuit base – my favourite flavour to use is cookies and cream. I usually add 1–2 dessertspoons as I like my ice cream sandwiches to be nice and fat. Top with another biscuit and then, using the back of a warmed teaspoon, smooth around the edge of the ice cream, so the side looks neat and flush with the biscuits. Pop the ice cream sandwich on a tray in the freezer and then repeat!

If you leave your ice cream sandwiches in the freezer for 48 hours, the biscuits will soften nicely, which makes them easier to eat and even more delicious.

You can also pimp your ice cream sandwiches by rolling the sides in sprinkles, nuts or chocolate chips. Easy!

Here's a thought … for an adults-only version, pour some brandy into a spray bottle and spritz over your biscuits before popping your ice cream sandwiches in the freezer.

Confidence in the kitchen means using store-bought ingredients with pride. There's no shame in using a supermarket sponge! I'm going to show you how to turn simple ingredients into a delicious dessert that's both homely and heartfelt. This recipe is inspired by a traditional Uruguayan cake. I've deconstructed it so your guests can dig around their dish to find the hidden jewels of meringue and dulce de leche. I love the fresh hit of mango, the saltiness of the peanuts and that beautiful whipped cream tying it all together.

CHAJA MESS

Serves 10–12

300 ml thickened cream, lightly whipped
2 store-bought sponge cakes, broken into large pieces (see tip)
400 g can dulce de leche
200 g salted roasted peanuts, chopped
2 x 400 g cans mango cheeks or slices (or use the cheeks from 2 large mangoes when in season)
4 large meringues (store bought are fine)
freeze-dried raspberry powder, to serve (optional; see tip)

We are going to be constructing this dessert a bit like an Eton mess. You'll need a large wooden board to assemble it on and a nice big serving spoon.

Scoop up a heap of fluffy whipped cream and dollop it on your serving board. Place a few more dollops on the board, then get the back of your spoon and spread the cream out with some big firm whacks! Save the rest of the cream for later on.

Arrange the pieces of sponge on top of the cream, then dollop on spoonfuls of dulce de leche, creating little caramel pockets. Scatter over the peanuts for some salt and crunch, then delicately lay the mango cheeks over the top. Top with dollops of the remaining cream, then crumble the meringues over to add some beautiful sweet crunch. For a lovely finishing touch, you can sprinkle a little freeze-dried raspberry powder over the top.

Take to the table and serve. This is one of those desserts that will be remembered and recreated for years to come!

tip

I often bake some of the sponge pieces in a 180°C oven for 10–15 minutes to give them a golden colour and a bit of firmness.

When assembling this dessert, I find it looks better if you break the sponge into large portions instead of crumbling it into little pieces on the plate.

Freeze-dried raspberry powder is available from gourmet food stores and some health food stores.

We would often eat this pie for afternoon tea when I worked at Endeavour Hills Pharmacy shortly after moving to Melbourne. I absolutely loved bringing in baked goodies for the ladies, who were from a generation that really appreciated a good morning tea. We'd chat and swap recipes, which is how I came upon this total gem. And now I'm going to share it with you! It is so simple and delicious that you should absolutely bake this today and take it into the office for afternoon tea tomorrow. It's what the ladies from Endeavour Hills Pharmacy would want!

LEMON MERINGUE PIE

Serves 10–12

200 g plain biscuits
100 g ginger snap biscuits
½ teaspoon ground or freshly grated nutmeg
150 g butter, melted
whipped cream, to serve

LEMON FILLING

2 x 395 g cans sweetened condensed milk
3 egg yolks
finely grated zest and juice of 1 lemon (you should get about 3 tablespoons of juice)

MERINGUE

3 egg whites
165 g (¾ cup) caster sugar

tip

To give extra oomph and height to your tart as we have done, just increase the quantity of meringue. For each extra egg white, you'll need to add 3 tablespoons of sugar.

I know they might not be the most everyday piece of kitchen equipment, but blow torches are so much fun to use. You can buy them from kitchenware or hardware stores and I can guarantee your guests will be impressed when you whip it out to brown the top of this baby! However, if you don't have a blow torch, you can pop the tart back in the oven for 10 minutes or until golden.

Grease a 20 cm cake tin or pie tin.

While the biscuits are still in the packet, smash them with a rolling pin to a reasonably fine crumb. Tip the biscuit crumb into a mixing bowl, add the nutmeg and melted butter and stir to combine well. Press it into the base of the prepared tin, curving it up the side a little bit, ready to hold the yummy lemon filling. Pop it in the fridge to set for 20 minutes or so.

Preheat the oven to 180°C.

To make the lemon filling, combine all the ingredients in a bowl until lovely and smooth. Pour into the tin and bake for 25 minutes. Remove from the oven and place in the fridge to chill.

While it's chilling, get on with the meringue. Using a stand mixer with the whisk attachment or electric beaters, beat the egg whites until stiff peaks form, then gradually beat in the sugar until you have yourself a nice gloss meringue.

Take the tart out of the fridge and spread the meringue mixture on top, making sure you give it as much volume as you can (see tip). Use your spatula to create little peaks and troughs to give your pie a proper swagger!

Now here comes the fun part. Grab a blow torch (see tip) and use it to create golden peaks on your pie. Set aside for 1 hour to set, then slice and enjoy with lashings of freshly whipped cream.

This recipe belongs to my big sister, Treena, and I feel so privileged to be sharing it in my first cookbook. Treena has been making her crème caramel for as long as I can remember. She has always cooked it from memory, and has never measured an ingredient or written down the method until now. It's beautiful, generous and always puts a smile on people's faces. Just like Treena.

Treena's CRÈME CARAMEL

Serves 8

100 g caster sugar

CUSTARD

600 ml pouring cream
1 large egg
5 large egg yolks
3 pinches of sea salt
165 g (¾ cup) caster sugar
1 teaspoon vanilla bean paste

Preheat the oven to 160°C.

Place the sugar and 1½ tablespoons of water in a small, heavy-based saucepan over medium heat and cook slowly, without stirring, until it turns a medium to dark brown. The caramel will become more bitter as it continues to darken so take it as far as your taste dictates (my sister likes hers nice and bitter and it tastes divine with the rich baked custard). Pour the caramel into an 18 cm baking dish.

Now for the custard. Pour the cream into a saucepan over medium heat and heat just until you see bubbles forming around the edge. Do not let it boil!

Place the egg, egg yolks and salt in a large bowl and whisk for 30 seconds. Add the sugar and vanilla and continue whisking until it has nearly dissolved. While still whisking, gradually add the warm cream. Keep going until the sugar has completely dissolved.

Strain the custard through a sieve over the caramel in the baking dish and cover with foil. Pop the dish into a large roasting tin and pour enough water into the tin to come half way up the side of the dish. Bake for 40 minutes, then turn off the heat and leave in the oven to cool for 1 hour.

Pop the crème caramel in the fridge to completely set overnight. To serve, remove the foil and place a large serving plate over the caramel dish. Now, with a quick flick and a little confidence (you got this!), invert the plate and dish so the caramel is sitting the right way up on the plate. Gently remove the dish, cut the crème caramel into slices or scoop spoonfuls into bowls and serve.

Dress up some store-bought brownies and take a load off with these gorgeous drunken cherries. Toast your brownies in a sandwich grill or pop them in the oven for 10 minutes to warm slightly, then spoon over the cherries and light up your table.

CHOCOLATE BROWNIES *with* DRUNKEN CHERRIES

Makes 12

12 store-bought brownies of your choice
whipped cream, to serve

DRUNKEN CHERRIES
680 g jar morello cherries
2 tablespoons alcohol of your choice (flavoured vodka, amaretto and brandy all work well)
2½ tablespoons caster sugar
1 teaspoon vanilla extract

To make the drunken cherries, place a sieve over a small saucepan and drain the cherries, so that the liquid goes into the pan. Add the remaining ingredients to the pan and bring to the boil over high heat.

Boil for 20 minutes or until the liquid has reduced to a thick syrup. Add the cherries and give it a good stir.

Place the brownies on a serving platter and spoon the warm drunken cherries over the top. Serve with a big old bowl of whipped cream.

CAKES, BISCUITS *and* SLICES

Bloody good baked treats!

It's no secret that every market day you can find me down at the South Melbourne Market with a coffee in hand. If you've seen my Insta Stories, you'll know I always head to Canteen to see what Brad's got on offer. Some people window shop and drool over shoes. I window shop and drool over Brad's food, so it was only natural that I would ask him to be a part of this book, and he was generous enough to share this delicious recipe for his chocolate cheesecake brownies. Enjoy!

Chocolate cheesecake BROWNIES

Makes 24 pieces

- 400 g dark chocolate, broken into pieces
- 325 g unsalted butter, roughly chopped
- 6 eggs
- 2 egg yolks
- 300 g caster sugar
- 80 g cocoa powder
- 120 g plain flour
- pinch of sea salt

CHEESECAKE TOPPING

- 900 g cream cheese, softened
- 3 eggs
- 150 g caster sugar
- 1 teaspoon vanilla bean paste

Preheat the oven to 170°C. Line a 20 x 30 cm baking tin with baking paper, making sure the paper hangs over the edges of the tin. This will help you lift out the brownies when they're cooked.

Melt the chocolate and butter in a saucepan over low heat and mix until smooth. Remove from the heat and allow to cool slightly.

Using a stand mixer fitted with the whisk attachment, beat the eggs, egg yolks and sugar until light and fluffy. Add the cooled chocolate mixture, cocoa, flour and salt and mix to combine. Set aside.

To make the cheesecake topping, place all the ingredients in a large bowl and mix until smooth and sexy.

Pour the brownie mixture into the prepared tin and spread it out evenly, then pour the cheesecake mixture on top and smooth the surface.

Bake for 50 minutes or until just set. It should be ever so slightly wobbly in the middle, but it will finish setting as it cools. Set aside in the fridge to chill until completely set.

Cut the cheesecake into 24 slices (it's very rich, so a little goes a long way!) and enjoy.

The brownies will keep in an airtight container in the fridge for up to 2 days.

EMMYLOU'S LIFE HACKS

FROZEN BANANAS

These bad boys are extremely useful to have on hand for smoothies, pancakes, cakes and porridge, plus they're a great way to stop over-ripe bananas going to waste.

All you need to do is peel your bananas and place them on a baking tray lined with baking paper.

Pop the tray in the freezer and leave the bananas to freeze solid for 1–2 hours. Freezing them separately like this first will stop them from sticking together later on.

Transfer the frozen bananas to zip-lock bags and pop them back in the freezer. Easy!

You know how it is. One week your kids are crazy for bananas and the next week they won't touch them. Now you're stuck with a bunch of brown bananas and nothing for afternoon tea. No need to stress – just refer to my banana hack on page 193 and you've got the perfect excuse to bake this cake any time you want! The coconut cream makes it really moist and you can easily substitute the eggs for chia seed gel to make it vegan.

BANANA, COCONUT CREAM *and* DATE CAKE

Serves 12

225 g (1½ cups) plain flour
1 teaspoon baking powder
1 teaspoon bicarbonate of soda
½ teaspoon ground ginger
½ teaspoon ground cinnamon
½ teaspoon ground nutmeg
good pinch of sea salt
95 g (½ cup) firmly packed brown sugar
45 g (½ cup) desiccated coconut
270 ml can coconut cream
2 eggs (see tip)
3 large bananas, mashed, plus 2 bananas, halved lengthways, to decorate
1 teaspoon vanilla extract
5 large fresh or dried pitted dates (soak in warm water for an hour and drain if they are dried)

tip

If you would like to make a vegan version of this cake, simply replace the eggs with a chia seed gel. Place 2 tablespoons of chia seeds in a small bowl, add 125 ml (½ cup) of water and leave for 5 minutes to turn into a gel. That's it!

Preheat the oven to 180°C and line a 20 cm square tin with baking paper.

Combine the flour, baking powder, bicarb, ground spices, salt, sugar and desiccated coconut in a mixing bowl.

Place the remaining ingredients in a blender and blitz until smooth. Add to the dry ingredients and fold until just combined. Pour into the prepared tin and arrange the halved bananas on top.

Bake for 45 minutes or until golden and a skewer inserted in the centre comes out clean. Cool in the tin for a few minutes, then turn out onto a wire rack to cool.

Cut the cake into 12 slices and serve either warm or cold. Any leftovers will store in an airtight container in the fridge for up to 2 days.

This is another recipe from my brother Kim-Lee. I guarantee the kids will be happy to help you make this one! There is no right or wrong here so you can change the quantities if you want more of a chocolate texture or marshmallow taste.

Unbelievably DREAMY ROCKY ROAD

Makes 18 pieces

500 g white chocolate, broken into pieces
100 g red raspberry lollies, halved
100 g shortbread biscuits, roughly chopped
100 g mini marshmallows
100 g macadamias, roughly chopped
40 g desiccated coconut

tip

The recipe says to cut the rocky road into bars, but you could also break it into uneven pieces for a more rustic look.

Dollop the mixture into sexy paper cases for parties.

You can swap the white chocolate for dark or milk chocolate if you want a more traditional rocky road flavour.

Line a 20 cm square cake tin with baking paper.

Melt the chocolate in a heatproof bowl set over a saucepan of simmering water (make sure the base of the bowl doesn't touch the water). Stir it regularly to make sure it doesn't overheat. When the chocolate is smooth with no lumps remaining, remove the bowl from the heat and set aside.

Combine the raspberry lollies, biscuits, marshmallows, macadamias and 3 tablespoons of the desiccated coconut in a large bowl. Pour the melted chocolate over the top and fold gently until all the dry ingredients are coated.

Pour the mixture into the prepared tin and smooth the surface. Sprinkle over the remaining coconut, then pop it in the fridge for 2 hours to set.

Cut into 18 bars to serve. Any leftovers will keep in an airtight container in the fridge for up to 1 week.

MAKE YOUR OWN CAKE STAND

Cakes always look amazing when placed on a fancy cake stand, but the stands can be pretty expensive, so I decided to make my own for a fraction of the price. All you need is a visit to your local op-shop and some epoxy glue from your local hardware store. Here's how to do it.

Head to your nearest op-shop or second-hand store and trawl the glassware section. You're looking for a wide-rimmed shallow glass and a decorative plate. The glass will become your cake stand base and the plate will become the top.

To put the stand together, turn the glass and plate upside down. Squeeze a line of epoxy glue around the base of the glass, then turn it over and press it in the middle of the overturned plate. Gently press for 1–2 minutes to help the glue stick then set aside, upside-down, for a few hours until completely set.

Turn the cake stand over and there you have it! A completely unique cake stand for no more than a couple of dollars.

What's the best thing about a party when you're a guest? The cake. What's the worst thing about a party when you're a host? The cake. If you're not confident in the kitchen, a cake can be your undoing. It's the one thing that you're bound to end up in tears over. But my celebration cake is here to save the day! It's the easiest way to impress your guests without all the stress. You're basically taking a store-bought packet mix and pimping it up with a few simple hacks. When it comes to the cake itself, you can choose whatever floats your boat, though I must say I love vanilla as it looks spectacular, keeps well and is a lovely rich cake to work with.

CELEBRATION CAKE

Serves a crowd

2 packets of your favourite cake mix
250 g packet shortbread biscuits, crushed to a rubble

LIQUID GOLD

395 g can sweetened condensed milk
250 ml (1 cup) evaporated milk

CREAM CHEESE FROSTING

500 g cream cheese, softened
180 g unsalted butter, softened
180 g icing sugar, sifted
1 teaspoon vanilla bean extract or paste

Make a double batch of your favourite cake mix following the packet instructions. Divide between two greased and lined 20 cm cake tins and bake as directed. When they're ready, get them out of the oven and let them cool in the tins for a few minutes, then turn them out onto a wire rack to cool completely. If you're making them ahead of time, store the cooled cakes in the fridge until you're ready to decorate them.

To make the liquid gold, mix the ingredients in a bowl. Easy.

For the frosting, beat all the ingredients using hand-held beaters or a stand mixer fitted with the paddle attachment. You want it to be super smooth and creamy.

Grab your cakes and, if you're feeling game, cut each one in half horizontally. Otherwise two layers of cake are fine. Place one piece of cake on a platter or cake stand. Pour over a little liquid gold, followed by a good smear of frosting and some shortbread crumbs. Add the next cake layer and repeat the process as many times as required, depending on how many layers you have. For a nude cake, simply add the last of the frosting to the top. Or for that extra love, make a batch of buttercream icing (see below) and generously ice the entire cake.

Now it's time for the fun part – decorating! All white is very glam or you may want to go all out with colour. See the following spread for ideas.

Buttercream icing

Makes enough to ice a large cake

250 g unsalted butter, softened
685 g (5½ cups) icing sugar, sifted
1 teaspoon vanilla bean extract or paste
1–2 tablespoons milk
a few drops of food colouring of your choice (optional)

Using a stand mixer fitted with the paddle attachment, beat the butter until pale and creamy. When I say pale and creamy it really needs to change colour, so give yourself a good 8–10 minutes.

Grab a dessertspoon and start adding the icing sugar a spoonful at a time. Slow the mixer down with every addition, then beat a little faster to help it dissolve into the butter. When you are down to your last cup of icing sugar, add the vanilla, 1 tablespoon of milk and food colouring (if using). Spoon in the last of the icing sugar and beat for a further 3 minutes, adding the rest of the milk if you need it. You want this icing to be beautifully fluffy.

EMMYLOU
LOVES
YOU

TIME TO DECORATE!

- Use old-school lollies like bananas or raspberries to make a striking graphic pattern.
- Use my dreamy rocky road (see page 200) instead of shortbread crumbs to fill the centre of your cake, then pile some big chunks on top.
- Store-bought cake toppers, macarons, mini gingerbread houses, pressed edible flowers, even little animals from the $2 shop can all look fabulous.
- For a floral pattern, cut pink marshmallows in half to create petals and use pink Smarties for the centre.
- Using hundreds and thousands in all their glory is a simple idea that works really well.

EMMYLOU
LOVES
YOU

CONVERSION CHARTS

Measuring cups and spoons may vary slightly from one country to another, but the difference is generally not enough to affect a recipe. All cup and spoon measures are level.

One Australian metric measuring cup holds 250 ml (8 fl oz), one Australian tablespoon holds 20 ml (4 teaspoons) and one Australian metric teaspoon holds 5 ml. North America, New Zealand and the UK use a 15 ml (3-teaspoon) tablespoon.

LENGTH

METRIC	IMPERIAL
3 mm	⅛ inch
6 mm	¼ inch
1 cm	½ inch
2.5 cm	1 inch
5 cm	2 inches
18 cm	7 inches
20 cm	8 inches
23 cm	9 inches
25 cm	10 inches
30 cm	12 inches

LIQUID MEASURES

ONE AMERICAN PINT	ONE IMPERIAL PINT
500 ml (16 fl oz)	600 ml (20 fl oz)

CUP	METRIC	IMPERIAL
⅛ cup	30 ml	1 fl oz
¼ cup	60 ml	2 fl oz
⅓ cup	80 ml	2½ fl oz
½ cup	125 ml	4 fl oz
⅔ cup	160 ml	5 fl oz
¾ cup	180 ml	6 fl oz
1 cup	250 ml	8 fl oz
2 cups	500 ml	16 fl oz
2¼ cups	560 ml	20 fl oz
4 cups	1 litre	32 fl oz

DRY MEASURES

The most accurate way to measure dry ingredients is to weigh them. However, if using a cup, add the ingredient loosely to the cup and level with a knife; don't compact the ingredient unless the recipe requests 'firmly packed'.

METRIC	IMPERIAL
15 g	½ oz
30 g	1 oz
60 g	2 oz
125 g	4 oz (¼ lb)
185 g	6 oz
250 g	8 oz (½ lb)
375 g	12 oz (¾ lb)
500 g	16 oz (1 lb)
1 kg	32 oz (2 lb)

OVEN TEMPERATURES

CELSIUS	FAHRENHEIT
100°C	200°F
120°C	250°F
150°C	300°F
160°C	325°F
180°C	350°F
200°C	400°F
220°C	425°F

CELSIUS	GAS MARK
110°C	¼
130°C	½
140°C	1
150°C	2
170°C	3
180°C	4
190°C	5
200°C	6
220°C	7
230°C	8
240°C	9
250°C	10

THANK YOU!

This is a massive shout out to all the people in my tribe who have brought this book to life.

Firstly, to Kellie Joy Bright. It was so much fun sharing my stories with you. I am truly grateful to have such an old friend help me bring them to life on paper. We have come a long way since living in our Geelong share house, working together at Bell Post Hill Pharmacy and living on nothing but pizza and sushi!

To my beautiful mum Phuong, my dad Kim, my two brothers Kim-Lee and Khanh, and my sisters Sue-Lyn and Treena. Without our colourful life, which at times was so hard we thought we would never get through it, my character would not have been built in the way it has been. I appreciate every one of you, our dark times, our light times and all of the adventures that are still to come.

Aaron Love, you have supported me more than anyone else, and over the last 10 years we have created a beautiful family which you let me share with the world. From the bottom of my heart, I thank you.

To my children, who have given me an understanding of love that I didn't know existed. Sage, you are every bit as wise as your name suggests and I am so proud of the young man you are. Camellia, my first-born little girl. Your pure heart, the strength you have in your bones and soul will always take my breath away. Vida, my little baby who has the character of all of us. You, my girl, are pure joy, we are all so grateful for how much you teach us about love.

To the crew at South Melbourne Market. One of my greatest joys is continuing to grow my community within the market and I am so proud to watch all the businesses grow together.

To the incredible creative team who brought this book to life. Kirby Armstrong, the design of this book is just stunning. Thank you! Mark Roper, it was a pleasure to work with you, thank you for your beautiful photos. To Lee Blaylock and Rachel Vigor, you are both incredible stylists. Your work was superb. To the super talented chefs who cooked all the food in the book, Caroline Griffiths, Sarah Watson and Emma Warren – thank you! A big thank you, also, to my wonderful recipe editors, Rachel Carter and Lucy Heaver.

To Mary Small, Jane Winning and the whole team at Plum/Pan Macmillan, thank you for believing in me and my community and letting me share my vision and recipes with the world.

To Colin Fassnidge and Siba Mtongana – two incredible chefs I have learned so much from – for being so generous and allowing me to include one of your recipes in my book.

Lastly, to my community. You let me into your homes, allow me to cook in front of you, trust me enough to give my recipes a go and, more importantly, share and pass on the knowledge to create your own communities and memories.

EMMYLOU
LOVES

KAWARAU BRIDGE BUNGY 43M

INDEX

T

U

V

W

Z